IT IS TIME TO ELEVATE!

GETTING BACK TO THE BASICS

Seven Principles for Elevating the Family

Rex Tonkins

WESTBOW
PRESS®
A DIVISION OF THOMAS NELSON
& ZONDERVAN

WestBow Press books may be ordered through booksellers or by contacting:

WestBow Press
A Division of Thomas Nelson & Zondervan
1663 Liberty Drive
Bloomington, IN 47403
www.westbowpress.com
844-714-3454

ISBN: 978-1-6642-3413-0 (sc)
ISBN: 978-1-6642-3414-7 (e)

Print information available on the last page.

WestBow Press rev. date: 06/01/2021

For my wife, Vickie. Thank you for your relentless support for more than three decades. You have been a faithful and loyal friend to me through every season we have faced. As I walk with God's grace, I am blessed to have a wife who is a bright, beautiful, and brilliant woman of God.

I am blessed with two beautiful children, Christian and Victoria, and they both have blessed me with a growing family. Christian and his wife, Elle, have blessed me with two grandchildren, Ruthie and Iris. Victoria and her husband, Nelson, have blessed me with two grandchildren, Samantha Joy and Nelson III.

I also want to thank our good friend Heather George for her dedication in editing and preparing this book for publication.

CONTENTS

ENDORSEMENTS

The greatest endowment for your children and grandchildren can't be deposited in a bank. It can't be sold or traded or borrowed. It is an unshakable heritage of faith. It is the only gift that will stand the test of time. Everything else will fade away. Only by introducing your sons and daughters to Jesus Christ will you help them secure eternal life. How is that accomplished? By starting early and being intentional about the spiritual training of your children. It won't happen if left to chance.

—Dr. James Dobson, *Your Legacy: The Greatest Gift*

Every person receives a heritage, good or bad. It is comprised of a spiritual, social, and emotional legacy. The key is to be intentional in understanding what and how to pass your values and beliefs to those in your spheres of influence. This mission starts right in your home.

The foundational biblical understanding, found in Deuteronomy 6:4–7 (NIV), is that parents are responsible for the spiritual training of children. God created the family as the primary "institution" to pass the faith to the next generation. "Teach [my commandments] to your children" (Deuteronomy 4:9; 11:19 NIV). Most of us, however, feel inadequate and ill-equipped when it comes to creating a God-honoring home environment. This is where leadership training comes in, and that is what you are holding in your hands. These seven principles for elevating the family are going to equip you to establish a firm foundation of faith in your home, and these timeless axioms will carry over into the world around you.

Like it or not, you are faced with the realization that, for good or bad, parents influence the lives of future generations in ways they can't even imagine. No pressure—it's all part of the job!

Through the progression from diapers to diplomas, there is one overarching issue that confronts every Christian parent: the spiritual growth of our children.

> Train a child in the way he should go, and
> when he is old he will not turn from it.
> (Proverbs 22:6 NIV)

When we read this scripture, we realize that we're not all clear on what that means. We have promised ourselves that we will not make the same mistakes that our parents made with us, but beyond that, we were most likely hard-pressed to come up with a clear, coherent, biblical statement of what is involved in training up our children in the ways they should go.

Why do we need to be intentional? Some studies have shown that as many as 70 percent of young people raised in church have not embraced the faith as their own by the time they graduate from high school. Your children must learn and see the truth modeled by you. Parents are the most influential people in their children's lives.

The real encouragement for parents is that we don't need to spend time worrying about how we are going to accomplish this huge task. We just need to concentrate on one little picture at a time, and God will take care of the big picture. How can you intentionally create those individual snapshots in your child's life? Very simply, we need to give our children three things: an unshakeable foundation, an internal line, and an understanding of biblical principles.

When you take the time to introduce your family to Jesus by leading and serving like Him, you're laying an unshakable foundation for their lives. The sure foundation for your children's lives is Jesus Christ.

> Lay up treasure for themselves as a firm foundation for the coming age, so that they may take hold of the life that is truly life. (1 Timothy 6:19 NIV)

All parents know intuitively that our children need moral and ethical boundaries. They need lines of behavior that don't waver or change based upon opinion polls. They need godly character standards that can guide and direct them away from sin and toward God's best. Lines of righteousness add meaning and purpose to a child's life.

When we spiritually train our children, we are preparing them for life—and not just for guilt-free church attendance:

> Fathers, do not exasperate your children; instead, bring them up in the training and instruction of the Lord. (Ephesians 6:4 NIV)

Spiritual training is not an add-on; it forms the core of your family structure and your child's being and life. The spiritual training of our children should be the foundation of our parenting, handing over to our children the truths and principles that explain and govern life itself.

You can learn the rules and details of how to play baseball from a book or have someone explain them to you, but until you have someone physically and practically show you how to play the game and start practicing, everything you know is just theory. The Bible instructs parents to teach our children about God and the Christian life and to show them how to live it out by example and training.

That is what this book is all about. It is time to elevate! These seven principles for elevating the family are going to equip you to pass a legacy of faith!

—Dr. John Bornschein

It is a great honor to recommend a book, but it is even a greater one to endorse the individual who has written the book. Rex Tonkins brings credibility and integrity to what he puts on paper. We have known the Tonkins family for many years and have encountered and enjoyed their friendship in our home and church. They are the real deal! This book is not just another ethereal treatise on a topic that might catch your eye. Coach Rex writes with honesty and transparency as he unfolds biblical principles that help elevate individuals to a higher level of living and leadership. As you read this book, you will relate and connect with a man of God in real life and the Word of God. Be strengthened and encouraged as you dive into a book that runs contrary to the world's culture and is aligned with God's ideal.

—Pastor Tom J. Perea, lead pastor of
Restoration Fellowship International

It Is Time to Elevate is a book for the time in which we live. Rex Tonkins, affectionately known as "Coach Rex," has hit the nail on the head in dealing with critical issues and exposing the deception designed by the accuser of the brethren, the adversary of the Christian faith, and the hater of everything holy, sacred, and righteous in our past, present and future as people: the devil! From the beginning, Satan has sought to destroy the image of God on the earth: the nuclear family.

Today, I thank God for raising up a voice and a defender of the family in the person of His servant leader, Rex Tonkins. Coach Rex has stood and continues to stand uncompromisingly upon the wall of the Word of God as one of the Lord's end-time watchmen to sound the alarm and warn families throughout our culture of the enemy's advance and strategy of attack against God's bedrock in society: the family.

Coach Rex treads out the grain of scriptures of the Holy Bible and teaches timeless, proven principles for success in the family. He exposes the deception and lies of the devil and draws a clear road map to God's way of success through the Holy Bible.

Rex incorporates practical examples, patriarchal testimonials, and personal experiences from his more than thirty years of marriage and fatherhood. This proud grandparent has shared a blueprint for building our homes according to God's specifications and design so that our labor as husbands, wives, and children is not in vain!

It Is Time to Elevate is must read for every Christian, male and female, single or married, because it straightens the error of past destructive decisions and dynamics that lead to patterns of failure within the family, it strengthens the resolve of those who are striving to set the proper order within the family, and it supports those who are on the path of Truth in building their families according to God's instruction to continue elevating with much energy, effort, and enthusiasm.

—Dr. Christopher A. Stone, senior pastor, Unity Worship Center C.O.G.I.C. Burlington, North Carolina

Every follower of Christ needs to be regularly encouraged and instructed to go higher and further in accomplishing God's purpose for their life. Coach Rex has invested his life in serving others in that way. His latest book, *It Is Time to Elevate*, provides motivation and insight to elevate and integrate your walk with God, your relationships, your work, and your ministry. The book is filled with memorable stories and experiences from Rex's life, and each chapter includes pertinent scriptures, practical applications, biblical prayers and declarations, and questions to ponder. I highly recommend *It Is Time to Elevate*.

—Dr. Todd Hudnall, senior pastor,
Radiant Church, Colorado Springs

INTRODUCTION

Elevate means to exalt, or to make exceedingly high. The Greek word for elevate is *hupsoo*, which means to lift or raise up, to exalt, or to lift the hand. This involves prioritizing or ranking over.

> Seek the kingdom of God, above all else, and live righteously and He will give you everything you need. (Matthew 6:33 NLT)

This verse is simply telling us to search for God's righteousness, peace, and joy through the Holy Spirit. I challenge you to search for the amazing secrets and keys to the kingdom so that you can unlock the mysteries of what God has planned for your life. Put prayer and study at the top position and keep it high on your daily priority list.

How many times do we look outside and blame the ills of society on other people and other institutions? What are we doing to make a difference in our own homes?

> For the time has come for judgment (condemning wrongful behavior) and it must begin with God's household, And if judgment begins with us, what terrible fate awaits those who have never obeyed God's Good News?" (1 Peter 4:17 NLT)

We must return to God's foundational plan for the family. It is time for the people who follow God to step up, step in, and step out into God's plan and purpose to advance His kingdom on the earth. This book is designed to teach you how to fight for your marriage and family.

Nehemiah understood the urgency of his time and rallied the people of God to make a stand and fight.

> Then as I looked (perceived) over the situation, I called together the nobles and the rest of the people and said to them, "Don't be afraid of the enemy! Remember the Lord, who is great and glorious, and fight for your brothers, your sons, your daughters, your wives, and your homes!" (Nehemiah 4:14 NLT)

The intentional plan of Satan is to completely disfigure the family because the family consists of a husband and wife and children, which is the very essence and image of God. Satan has used pride, temptation, entertainment, government, and education as puppets to do his wickedness against the family.

We must come to understand the bigger picture of how to utilize our spiritual weapons of God's Word to stop and defeat the enemy and his evil agenda. We do this by living righteous, holy lives in Christ, studying the blueprint of life—the Bible— and declaring His Word over our lives and our families.

I am the first to say that my very own family has had our share of problems and mistakes. I have had my share of personal challenges and struggles, but God has been faithful to me and has favored me to do many awesome things I do not deserve. I know that I am what I am simply by the grace of God. In writing books, I am simply obeying what I believe

God has inspired me to do and pointing people to biblical principles that are proven to bring success if they are followed by faith and prayer. I will be transparent in sharing the good, bad, and ugly moments of my life as a husband, father, and leader. I will share testimony of my family's victories and how the grace of God has brought us through each trial and valley with mercy and grace.

Entering this book will inspire you to step up and fight for what is right. You will become hungry to step into God's ultimate plan for your life and fulfill what you were born to do, which is to glorify God. When God's kingdom is ushered into the spheres of influence, lives will be changed and saved from destruction. You will learn strategic principles that are aligned in truth and facts and that will raise your thinking. Reading these biblical principles will help you be a better leader, a better husband to your wife—or wife to your husband—and a better parent to your children. It will also help children see the necessity of honoring their parents.

In this book, people of all ages will gain the understanding of how much God values their lives. I also will reveal the steps of how you can gain more insight into your very own purpose and be able to walk in the plan God has for you. The biblical principles in this book will help you unlock the leadership abilities that are within you. In this book, I will share the keys to putting your energy, enthusiasm, and effort into your divine assignment. I will unveil the values that are sacred and important to God that add longevity into your life and family. You will learn how to align yourself with God's agenda and advance and accelerate forward into your calling. This book will help you understand the key ingredients that are mixed with faith in God, and that will inevitably help you glorify the Lord, help you excel, leave a legacy of blessings, and finish strong in Christ Jesus.

As we can clearly see with the state of the family, times have changed drastically since the 1980s. God's original plan is still relevant for today and must continue to be implemented in every generation. We cannot allow cultural and societal trends to dictate to us anything different. God's way is the best way, and it has always been the best for the family.

> Today I have given you a choice between life and death, between blessing and curses. Now I call on heaven and earth to witness the choice you make. Oh, that you would choose life, so that you and your descendants might live. (Deuteronomy 30:19 NLT)

We must wake up and realize it is time to make a difference to help support future generations. Often busyness and fulfilling our appetites take precedence over the future and the destiny of the younger generation. We must be aware of the trappings that hurt the family, including the pride of life, the lust of the eyes, and the lust of the flesh. Instead, we must humble ourselves and recognize that we need God's help. We must get rid of selfish pride and selfish ambition and pursue the things that are eternal.

> In the beginning, God created male and female and God said, "Be fruitful and multiply." (Genesis 1:26–28 NLT)

The foundation of family is the male who produces seed and the female where seed can produce life. The Greek word for *male* means to lift, to bear up, and to pick up. The Greek word for female means to nurse and nurture. God's instructions for the male and female are to be fruitful, which means to have children, and multiply your influence.

The definition of the family is a group consisting of parents and children living in the same household. God's original plan and divine plan is that the household be a father and mother with children. The family in this order reveals what God is like. The Hebrew definition of "family" is a family or social unit including close and distant relatives or "mishpachah." The family is a group joined where each role in the family serves a specific function to keep the family together.

The legal definition means a group of individuals who share ties of blood, marriage, or adoption; a group residing together and consisting of parents, children, and other relatives by blood or marriage. The family has been jolted into something that is the opposite of God's original design. The family is the center of society, and when families are weak, society is weak. The purpose of the family is to be a safe and supportive base from which to explore the world.

God designed the family whereby the man discovers a wife who fits him, and the wife receives love the way she needs to be loved. God's order and design is for the husband and wife to submit to one another, recognizing the man as the head of the family. This does not mean one is superior to the other; it just means God gave more rank and authority to the husband to lead the family. Obviously, if a man of the home is not submitting to God and is causing chaos in his home, this is just cause for teaching, guidance, and accountability so that the man understands his role and position.

The word *submission* is portrayed as a negative word to some—some people think the word is an inferior word—but the word means to come up under as the general of an army. The soldiers are equal as people, but the general has the rank and authority to carry out divine orders. To have order in a home, authority must be understood to avoid confusion and division within the home. The husband and wife governing their home from biblical standards—praying together and tapping into each other's wisdom and perspectives—helps keep balance on a consistent basis, helping the environment to be full of love and unity within a home.

> There is no longer Jew or Gentile, slave or free, male or female. For you are all one in Christ Jesus. (Galatians 3:28 NLT)

God's ranking has things set up within the family so that the man is to lead his family. The man must be careful not to use his rank and authority to dominate the wife, and the wife must be careful that she does not try to control and manipulate the husband to get her own way. A husband cannot force his wife to submit; she must be willing. The husband is to love his wife, care for her, encourage her to grow in God, and serve her. A husband's love must be sacrificial in giving time, entertainment, friendship, and career in order to love his wife. The husband must be purposeful in teaching scripture, joining a Bible-preaching church, encouraging small groups so that his wife can grow and serve, and cultivating her character and her calling so she can fulfill God's purpose for her life. The husband must understand that he will answer to God in how he leads his family; this is why we must lead with humility and reverence.

Please understand that there is an intentional plan to destroy the nuclear family. The father figure is constantly bombarded with messages that the father is incompetent and clueless. The mother is portrayed as tough and rough, and the children are given gadgets to keep them entertained all day long, promoting an atmosphere that is not conducive for training and instructions of life skills, work ethic, and communication.

God has a divine order He set up in the beginning, and that order is for the man who has a family to lead and train his family in the ways and principles of the Lord. The woman is to help him in these endeavors with the buildup of the family. The wife is to support and respect her husband, and the husband is to love his wife, respect, and lay down time and effort to meet her needs.

The children must be taught the importance of honoring and respecting their parents because this pleases God. He has promised long life to those who honor their parents. The culture of America is trying to make things backward by pushing an agenda that children should not listen to their parents, insisting that they don't know what they are talking about. Husbands are portrayed as weak and passive men who allow things to happen that go against biblical standards. Wives are portrayed as the dominant and tough ones who lead their families.

Every member in the family has a vital role that is important to the success of the family. Those roles have been clearly defined in scripture. Sadly, men are marginalized and downtrodden so often by the media and culture that they just want to check out because of so many subliminal messages. Men become passive and allow things to happen that go against their convictions and biblical standards.

When a man speaks up, he is slapped by the culture as being too hard and masculine. Therefore, the culture attempts to silence the voice of men across America. The culture wants men to act feminine and the women to act like men. The children are taught to be whatever gender they desire, causing mass confusion and destruction to the nuclear family.

Divorce in America has become an epidemic, and men and

women are giving up on each other. Men do not understand how to love and care for women. This leads to the woman despising and having no respect for her husband, causing the feelings of no value, being underappreciated, and having no desire to meet his needs as a man.

When the husband and the wife are not meeting each other's needs, their children are missing out on seeing what it means to have healthy relationships. The children become confused about their identities and purposes because the parents are not showing them the proper way of functioning within a family.

Feminism is at an all-time high; unfortunately, the fuel behind feminism is the insecurity and abuse of dominating males who do not understand their roles as providers, protectors, and encouragers who help empower their wives. Most women have no problem following a man who is willing to lay down his life for his wife, cherish her, and not deal with her treacherously. Obviously, there are exceptions where the husband is doing everything necessary to be supportive—and the wife is doing everything necessary as his wife—but things don't always work out because people's hearts become hurt—and Satan gets a foothold after years of unhealthy relationships.

Unknown iniquities and generational curses are handed down from to one generation to another. Past generations roll down the pike, affecting innocent families, and not realizing a curse from previous generations has affected the family dynamic. The family is the foundation and the success of a nation.

Why does the family's purpose and roles appear to be eroding from their original purpose? It all comes from a devilish and demonic agenda produced by Satan himself. His goal is to kill, steal, and destroy anything that has been created in the image of God. Satan takes what God created to be beautiful and wonderful and warps it with abuse and destruction, targeting the precious human soul.

God created sex to produce children, to provide pleasure for both husband and wife, and to clearly identify the roles, characteristics, and personalities of each person. Men are born to hunt and pursue, and women are born to receive and be nurtured and cherished. In this book, we are going to learn seven timeless principles that will help the family remain vibrant and strong. Let's get ready to dive into the seven steps to elevating the family. We will go deeper into the foundation of the family and look at unbiblical mindsets that have decimated the family.

I was recently working a construction project in Arlington, Texas. We had to go into a muddy, smelly, and dirty pit to demolish old, outdated concrete and then reconstruct, fix, and update the pit. While in the process, we ran into a problem with water gushing, which caused a bigger problem. We had to stop the water before we could proceed with the project. Engineers and maintenance teams began looking for the source and root cause of the gushing water and shut it off. Once we were able to shut down the root cause, we were able to start reconstruction.

Our foundation and thought structures of what a family is must be reconstructed, aligned, and balanced according to God's design. We live in a sinful world, and we came from parents who also sinned. Patterns of the family have been passed down to us—some good and some bad. Everyone is guilty of sin, and some things we did in our lives are shameful. No one wants to talk about shameful actions and deeds because of the embarrassment they bring.

At the construction project, before we could finish cleaning up the area and reconstructing a better design, we had to get to the root of the water source that had caused the influx of water and mud. It is time to give the shame and pain to Jesus and allow Jesus to wash and cleanse us of the pain and shame by His blood. It is time to stop trying to stuff thoughts down underneath the earthen recesses of our mind and soul. We must confess and acknowledge our past mistakes to allow God to heal us completely—to make us clean and whole.

It is time to put on the armor of light and take off darkness. If we submit ourselves to Jesus, He makes all things new. Once you have confronted the issues of your past, it is time to apply God's precious Word into everyday life by confession and declaration. We must saturate our souls with the scriptures and meditate on the scriptures day and night; over time, this will redeem and restore our souls and our thoughts.

Joshua 1:8 (NLT) tells us to meditate in the Word day and night so that you have good success. When we study God's Word, we construct healthy ways that help our well-being and our families. When childhood memories of awful things, fights, and arguments you witnessed appear, talk about it to the Lord and to your spouse and pray together so that the healing process will begin. Do not stuff it underground; bring it into the light.

Don't give up!

> They should always pray and never give up.
> (Luke 18:1 NLT)

My wife and I have felt like throwing in the towel with each other—in many seasons of life—but by the grace of God, we did not. Each person and every married couple must decide to follow God's divine way. We have a choice to follow God's way, and heaven and earth are watching to see what we will decide. The family has been under assault for many decades and appears to be getting worse with each successive era and decade.

When spiritual tornadoes rip through families in epidemic proportions, we have no other recourse but to turn to our Holy Father for help. There is an evil agenda to redefine marriage so that ungodliness can appear as normal. The immorality and ungodliness only lead to the erosion of the family. God's original plan is the best plan for the family—no matter how much the entertainment industry, government legislation, or Satan try to manipulate a lie through the systems that influence our nation. God's truth stands in every time, season, and generation. There are those who sit in positions of influence and attempt to adjust the truth to accommodate a lie.

> They traded the truth about God for a lie. So, they worshipped and served the things created instead of the creator himself, who is worthy of eternal praise! Amen. (Romans 1:25 NLT)

Because you do not like the truth or cannot handle the truth, it gives no one the right or authority to force lies and lifestyles on the minds of innocent children and people. No one gets away with wicked plans that are clearly an abomination to a Holy God. God made male and female—only two genders. Wicked leadership is using the public education system with an intentional agenda to teach ideals that oppose what the Bible says and go against the very nature of how each human has been created.

In our lifetimes, our goal should be to glorify God, fulfill His purpose for our lives, and advance God's kingdom by bringing His righteousness, joy, and peace into the spheres that influence the culture. When we shine and excel for God, we set up the opportunity to share God's love with people. We must bring divine order into our homes and the places where we have influence. We are to stand up for truth and expose wickedness. The world has infiltrated the home and the church. Christians and the church of Christ are supposed to infiltrate the world with the good news so that lost people can have an opportunity to know an awesome God and experience His amazing love.

ENTER

PRAYING, PLANNING, AND PLAYING TOGETHER

To get to your destination by plane, you must enter the plane; to excel in football, the ball needs to enter the end zone; to get a college degree, you must enter the classroom—and before answering God's call, we must enter private prayer.

> But when you pray, go away by yourself, shut the door behind you, and pray to your Father in private. Then Your Father, who sees everything, will reward you. (Matthew 6:6 NLT)

Seeking God has rewards such as protection, understanding people, and having prophetic insights. We must find a private place to communicate with God without distractions. And when we are faithful in doing this, we will see God's power in our lives publicly. If you are not aware, we are at war. The word "look" in Hebrew is "*ra'ah*," which means to perceive; we must perceive and discern, we must fight for family values, and we must fight for the destiny of future generations.

We have entered a new era, and it is vital that we learn and

1

see what God's plan is and how we are to execute that plan. The word "enter" means "go into." The goal is a continual entering into God's presence, understanding His will, and being in the position to fulfill His will.

> Keep on asking, and you will receive what you ask for. Keep on seeking, and you will find. Keep on knocking, and the door will be opened to you. (Matthew 7:7 NLT)

We must fervently seek to enter God's rest and discover His battle strategy. And once we get the download from heaven, we must align that plan with our hearts and our mouths. Our thinking must align with His will, His ways, and His Word.

> Then he said to me, "Speak a prophetic message to these bones and say, 'Dry bones, listen to the word of the Lord. This is what the sovereign Lord says: Look! I am going to put breath into you and make you live again. I will put flesh and muscles on you and cover you with skin. I will put breath into you and you will come to life. Then you will know that I am the Lord.'" (Ezekiel 37:4–6 NLT)

When we enter God's presence, vision is birthed into us. We must be prepared and learn what His vision is for our lives and then implement the principles of the kingdom to fulfill God's plan. One problem is fear and unbelief; we can clearly see these hinder our purposes. In the account with Gideon, in chapter 6 of the book of Judges, God called Gideon a mighty man of valor, and Gideon argued with God about this fact. God gave Gideon the ability to be a warrior, but it took time for Gideon to have faith in God and believe what God said about him. The second problem is us; we must see ourselves as the Father sees us and believe what He says about us.

The reality is that God requires our obedience, especially when He has clearly revealed His will to us.

> Not everyone who calls out to me, "Lord! Lord!" will enter the kingdom of heaven. Only those who actually do the will of my Father in heaven will enter. (Matthew 7:21 NLT)

Therefore, it is imperative that we obey God's Word, His will, and His ways so that we do not miss His divine plan or disobey His divine orders. When we understand who we are in God and what He has wired us to do, we will have the confidence and knowledge to be victorious.

> The Angel of the Lord appeared to him and said to him, and said, "Mighty hero, the LORD is with you." (Judges 6:12 NLT)

Once Gideon began believing God and obeying His instructions, he began to see divine intervention. The key to Gideon's success was going into each endeavor with his might and ability first, and then God would move supernaturally on his behalf. Gideon had to enter into agreement with God, discovering peace and purpose by communing with God. God wants to fix our thinking so that we are effective and successful in battle. We must learn and understand God's specific strategy before going into battle.

Allow God to show you His divine order. For example, the number seven, which means completion and perfection, has a divine order in God's kingdom. Oftentimes, it takes multiple times for us to get the point of what God is doing in us and showing us. Just because you failed multiple times does not mean you are supposed to quit; studies reveal it takes, at the very minimum, seven times to master a problem.

Here is what I have researched about the number seven. There are seven seas and seven mountains, and music is based on seven basic notes. Light is passed through a prism, and then it splits into seven parts, which is known by a famous abbreviation VIBGYOR, the rainbow colors of violet, indigo, blue, green, yellow, orange, and red. There are seven basic crystal systems in minerals. Even within the periodic table, we can observe seven levels of periodicity. Movie producers use seven categories in developing a movie: "A character has a problem, meets a guide who gives them a plan, and calls them to action, which helps them avoid failure and ends in success." This is called the *storyboard framework*. The Holy Bible is the master textbook of all sciences—be it physics, chemistry, or music.

The number seven occurs 287 times in the Old Testament, which includes the seven spirits as named in Isaiah 11:2 (NLT):

> And the Spirit of the LORD will rest on him—
> the Spirit of wisdom and understanding, the
> Spirit of counsel and might, the Spirit of
> knowledge and the fear of the LORD.

In Revelation 2 and 3 (NLT), seven letters are addressed to the seven churches in Asia Minor (modern-day Turkey); also mentioned in Revelation are seven stars, seven seals, seven trumpets, and seven dooms. Life operates in cycles of seven; every seven years, changes occur in the body; there are seven bones in our necks, multiples of seven bones (fourteen) in our faces and ankles, and seven holes in our heads. There are seven parables in the book of Matthew. There are seven mysteries in the New Testament, Abrahamic blessings were sevenfold, there are seven pillars of wisdom talked about in the book of Proverbs, and Elijah prayed seven times before a rain cloud appeared in 1 Kings 18:42–45 (NLT).

As we enter God's kingdom, we will discover a divine order that we have access to by the blood of Jesus Christ. We must appropriate the authority that has been endowed to us as kingdom citizens. Jesus taught us to pray:

> Pray like this: Our Father in heaven, may your name be kept holy. May your kingdom come soon. May your will be done on earth as it is in heaven. (Matthew 6:9 NLT)

We have the honor and responsibility of bringing His righteousness, peace, and joy to the earth. I remember asking the Lord, "What do you want me to do?" And God said to me through the scriptures in Acts 9:6 (NLT), "Now get up and go into the city, and you will be told what you must do."

With all our inadequacies and problems, we enter and seek to grab hold of His divine plan for our lives, and we must desire it as if we are entering a wrestling match. This match is called fervent prayer as Jacob did. He was serious, and he had an honest conversation with God:

> This left Jacob all alone in the camp, and a man came and wrestled with him until the dawn began to break. When the man saw that he would not win the match, he touched Jacob's hip and wrenched it out of its socket. Then the man said, "Let me go, for the dawn

5

is breaking!" But Jacob said, "I will not let you go unless you bless me." "What is your name?" the man asked. He replied, "Jacob." "Your name will no longer be Jacob," the man told him. "From now on you will be called Israel, because you have fought with God and with men and have won." In Genesis 32:24–28 (NLT)

Gideon was another leader who was completely transparent about how he felt about himself, and he found peace, purpose, and an amazing plan for victory in God. When we find peace, we can find purpose.

In 2018, I experienced some of the greatest moments of my time in ministry. I had amazing opportunities to share the Gospel on the same platform with Will Graham, the late Billy Graham's grandson, and I completed my third book. Amazing opportunities were opened for us—and then came the summer months.

That is when things turned into an all-out battle in the heat of Vickie's political campaign. The attacks and hits went to unimaginable levels. Incidents from our personal lives were published in the *Gazette*. Suddenly, we had to move from our home after five years of good standing, and there were unexpected financial challenges. We then had family challenges that were unlike any we had ever seen. The very essence of everything I held dear appeared to be crumbling right before my eyes. My faith was shaken to the core, and I was on the verge of retaliating in ways that would not be pleasing to God. I was failing in relationships with family, and we had longtime friends turning their backs on us.

After everything was said and done, we were behind the eight ball financially. We were on the verge of ruin, but God held us in His hands on His unshakable foundation. I felt like I was taking a nosedive into destruction, but instead, by the grace of God, we landed on the Rock found in Jesus Christ. I entered a desperate season of prayer and received answers from God, after asking desperate questions of Him. I had never thought those challenges would happen in my family, but they were. The Lord began to reveal to me the warfare in the highest levels of politics in our city, county, and state. I also came to the rude awakening that those I thought were true friends really were not—and those I believed were my inner circle attacked me with words and writings that shook me to the very core of my life.

The Lord revealed that I must stop internalizing and receiving into my heart the words that were spoken against us and stop becoming bitter and hurt. I was bleeding deeply from everything that was happening. The Father showed me that I must get my mind out of fear and get my faith back in Him. I began to speak and apply His Word over the circumstances through Isaiah 54:17 (NLT):

> But in that coming day no weapon turned against you will succeed. You will silence every voice raised up to accuse you. These benefits are enjoyed by the servants of the Lord; their vindication will come from me. I, the Lord, have spoken.

I had to get my mind and mouth in alignment with God's mighty Word. I learned in great pain the process of crying out to God. When we are facing painful experiences, God has a way of getting our undivided attention. The Lord revealed some hard things about my mindset, my outlook on life, and my attitude concerning anger.

Being away from my family at Christmas for the first time was awfully hard; working in a construction pit removing concrete to earn extra income is not what I had planned for myself either. I was on a revamp project in Arlington, Texas, at the General Motors plant. I worked with construction workers, ironworkers, carpenters, steelworkers, and equipment operators to remove steel and concrete from the pits in the Arlington plant for thirty-three consecutive days in twelve-hour shifts. We were cutting concrete in large squares and clamping them to an excavator or backhoe, and then we lifted them out of the deep and large pits.

Some areas would not come up as easily as others, and the operator of these huge, heavy machines would form it like a fist and pound the concrete over and over until it would come loose. They would attempt to lift it up and out, but while the pounding was happening, all my physical senses were engaged with the process. My eyes, ears, and feet could feel the ground shaking, and I sensed the smell of dirt, concrete, smoke, and dust getting into my mouth.

The Lord spoke to me and said, "You have had stubborn areas in your life that have been there since you were a child. You have felt entitled that you could get angry anytime, anywhere, anyhow—to anyone you wanted, but this is not right. I am now breaking up in you this kind of thinking, and I am helping you see what you look like through the leaders in this construction environment—to help you see how ugly and awful this kind of attitude and thinking is."

I began to see some of my wrongful mindsets in other supervisors and superintendents. I realized it was awful and ugly to behave like that, and I asked the Lord to help me repent from that kind of behavior in my leadership. God had to take me to the pits of pain and toil to help me be delivered from destructive thinking so that He could elevate me to the place

He had set aside for me. We cannot allow our past and present culture to dictate how God desires us to lead and love people. Our philosophy must be biblical, and our value systems must be aligned with God.

The man of the family needs a revelation of who God made him to be. We have a tremendous responsibility to lead and fulfill the purpose in which God has created us. The father is the foundation of the family. Man was created from the ground, symbolizing foundation. When the man has a covenant friendship with God, this positions the wife and children to be in divine order. When the man's relationship is right with God, spiritual blessings follow and flow down the chain of command.

> And Gideon built an altar there to the Lord
> and called it Yahweh-Shalom (which means
> "the Lord is peace"). The altar remains in
> Ophrah in the land of the clan of Abiezer to
> this day. (Judges 6:24 NLT)

Shalom means completeness, soundness, and peace. Purpose means a reason for something, knowing the purpose for which you exist is the foundation for leadership, and leadership is about serving Jesus Christ. Our Commander and King, Jesus, empowers us for kingdom service, and leadership is about inspiring others to fulfill their divine purpose in Christ and advancing God's kingdom.

Leaders must take biblical principles into the arenas where they are called to go. Our country is eroding morally because we have people in leadership positions who have no principles and carry their own agendas into their areas of influence. Too many leaders in public service and politics have lost their values and ethics. Sadly, a culture is being indoctrinated that says they can have wealth without working for it. We are living in an age where people have more knowledge but no foundation of character. Character is the bedrock of who we are in Christ and who God has made us to be. Men who truly desire to follow God must learn to work out their salvation with fear and trembling and acquire thankful hearts, recognizing the tremendous opportunity we have being in covenant with a Holy God. When we are living and manifesting God's Word into our lives, we are literally advancing His kingdom throughout the earth.

I have gained a new understanding of where I am going with my life. I have recognized and am recognizing the destructive habits that have hindered my effectiveness for decades. However, by the grace of God, I am learning to replace them with good and biblical habits. We must allow the Holy Spirit to heal and rehabilitate us and help us apply new ways of doing things. I had to learn and become knowledgeable about new, more effective ways of dealing with situations. I know it is inevitable that I will face situations and circumstances that will reveal if I have profoundly changed my approach in dealing with problems and pressures that are a part of life.

The General Motors plant experience revealed keys in helping me understand human behavior. The first takeaway was that I must remain cool and not be impulsive or react to someone's behavior when it is directed at me. Secondly, I have to stay calm so that I can keep a clear head and mind in responding to God's desires for me. I also need to keep myself together and not fall apart and throw everything I have learned out the door. The Lord told me if I followed these fundamentals, He would bring me through victoriously. Since that experience in Texas, I have lived and preached staying cool, calm, and collected, which has helped me have a totally different outlook in dealing with people. We can find multiple scriptures in Proverbs that speak into these matters.

- "Short-tempered people do foolish things, and schemers are hated" (Proverbs 14:17 NLT).
- "Sensible people control their temper; they earn respect by overlooking wrongs" (Proverbs 19:11 NLT).
- "Fools vent their anger, but the wise quietly hold it back" (Proverbs 29:11 NLT).
- "Better to be patient than powerful; better to have self-control than to conquer a city" (Proverbs 16:32 NLT).
- "A gentle answer deflects anger, but harsh words make tempers flare" (Proverbs 15:1 NLT).
- "Understand this, my dear brothers and sisters: You must all be quick to listen, slow to speak, and slow to get angry" (James 1:19 NLT).
- "Don't use foul or abusive language. Let everything you say be good and helpful, so that your words will be an encouragement to those who hear them" (Ephesians 4:29 NLT).

In closing this chapter, I want to challenge you to listen to what God said to Joshua in Joshua 1:9: "This is my command— be strong and courageous! Do not be afraid or discouraged. For the Lord your God is with you wherever you go" (NLT).

In looking into the Hebrew meaning in this verse, here is what I found. "I charge you to be strengthen, alert and brave. Do not break from fear nor be shattered from pressure but know God walks with you everywhere you go." As we endeavor to enter the places God calls us to, we can have confidence that He is with us. Realize that God is King, and the things He tells us to do are not suggestions but commands. We are clearly told to not be afraid but be confident. Therefore, go forth into the arena God sends you with great confidence in Jesus's name.

Seven Points of Success

1. Engage the issues of your heart to get to the heart of the matter.
2. Equip yourself with the Word of God to help you overcome problems and issues.
3. Empower yourself through prayer and study of the scriptures.
4. Enthusiasm must be cultivated daily to pursue your divine purpose.
5. Endurance is necessary to push through difficult challenges.
6. Evaluation of progress determines your progress: "good," "fair," or "needs improvement."
7. Encourage yourself in the Lord by waiting in God's presence for renewed strength.

Prayer points to pray out loud over yourself, your wife, and your family. We fight with the Word of God; our fight is not against flesh and blood.

- "Anyone who listens to my teaching and follows it is wise, like a person who builds a house on solid rock. Though the rain comes in torrents and the floodwaters rise and the winds beat against that house, it won't collapse because it is built on bedrock" (Matthew 7:24–25 NLT).
- "But if you refuse to serve the Lord, then choose today whom you will serve. Would you prefer the gods your ancestors served beyond the Euphrates? Or will it be

the gods of the Amorites in whose land you now live? But as for me and my family, we will serve the Lord" (Joshua 24:15 NLT).

- "I will teach all your children, and they will enjoy great peace. You will be secure under a government that is just and fair. Your enemies will stay far away. You will live in peace, and terror will not come near. If any nation comes to fight you, it is not because I sent them. Whoever attacks you will go down in defeat. I have created the blacksmith who fans the coals beneath the forge and makes the weapons of destruction. And I have created the armies that destroy. But in that coming day no weapon turned against you will succeed. You will silence every voice raised up to accuse you. These benefits are enjoyed by the servants of the LORD; their vindication will come from me. I, the LORD, have spoken" (Isaiah 54:13–17 NLT).

- "Those who live in the shelter of the Most High will find rest in the shadow of the Almighty" (Psalm 91:1 NLT).

- "A psalm of David. Praise the Lord who is my rock. He trains my hands for war and gives my fingers skill for battle" (Psalm 144:1 NLT).

- "A final word: Be strong in the Lord and in his mighty power. Put on all of God's armor so that you will be able to stand firm against the strategies of the devil. For we are not fighting against flesh and blood enemies, but against evil rulers and authorities of the unseen world, against mighty powers in this dark world, and against evil spirits in the heavenly places. Therefore, put on every piece of God's armor so you will be able to resist the enemy in the time of evil.

Then after the battle you will still be standing firm. Stand your ground, putting on the belt of truth and the body armor of God's righteousness. For shoes, put on peace that comes from the good News so that you will be fully prepared. In addition to all of these, hold up the shield of faith to stop the fiery arrows of the devil. Put on salvation as your helmet, and take the sword of the Spirit, which is the word of God. Pray in the Spirit at all times and on every occasion. Stay alert and be persistent in your prayers for all believers everywhere" (Ephesians 6:10–18 NLT).

Elevate Questions

1. What is the goal behind entering?
2. What does it mean to enter God's kingdom?
3. Why did Gideon have trouble identifying who he was in God?
4. What did Coach Rex learn about himself in the concrete pits of Arlington, Texas?
5. What did Gideon discover about God?
6. How did Gideon enter His purpose and become a mighty hero?
7. Why should we keep a calm, cool, and collected demeanor?

LEARN

LEARNING AND GROWING TOGETHER

Learning means to acquire knowledge and skill, and it also means to become competent and proficient in a subject matter. When we put the Word of God into our hearts and minds, we learn to elevate and excel into our divine purpose and destiny. Solomon asked God for wisdom so he could govern the people correctly. God was pleased to see a teachable spirit upon Solomon and blessed him with great divine wisdom.

> "Give me an understanding heart so that I can govern your people well and know the difference between right and wrong. For who by himself is able to govern this great people of yours?" The Lord was pleased that Solomon had asked for wisdom. So God replied, "Because you have asked for wisdom in governing my people with justice and have not asked for long life or wealth or the death of your enemies—I will give you what you asked for! I will give you a wise and

> understanding heart such as no one else has
> had or ever will have!" (1 Kings 3:9–12 NLT)

True leadership is recognizing that we need God's help to lead effectively.

By God's amazing grace and salvation, my friends Chris Stone and Darryl Moore and I were elevated out of the inner city and into realm of the kingdom, which has transformed our lives for His glory. We were so hungry to learn that we were willing to position ourselves under leaders so we could learn how to live for Jesus, lead with wisdom, and war spiritually. We were hungry to learn and discovered life in the scriptures. This has helped point us in a direction that has brought us life and purpose.

> Seek first the kingdom of God above all else,
> and live righteously, and He will give you
> everything you need. (Matthew 6:33 NLT)

Learning occurs when God's Word is applied in our everyday lives, which results in changes in our behaviors. Through the power of the Cross and practicing the Word of God in our daily lives, we have experienced major transformations in our lives. We have learned this through the warriors of the Bible, such as David, Daniel, and Esther. David was a true worshipper and defeated a huge enemy with a stone. Daniel prayed and interpreted dreams and was saved from lions. Esther had divine favor, was anointed with beauty, and was sensitive to fulfilling God's purpose. Esther was sent to the kingdom for such a time as this to deliver a nation. We must learn the art of leading ourselves and our families into fulfilling God's will, which are the steps to growing and maturing.

> My people are being destroyed because they
> don't know me. (Hosea 4:6 NLT)

In every marriage relationship, there are bound to be problems and pressures that are a part of life. Through God's Word, we gain knowledge and wisdom in how to work out our problems and differences. We must learn and apply God's principles to every area of our lives—to help overcome obstacles—especially in our relationships.

As we develop a deep relationship with the Lord, this will also help us maintain deep trust and intimacy with our spouses. We must never give up on our desire for unity and harmony in marriage relationships and in our homes. As mentioned in the introduction, there is an assault on the family. We must learn to apply ourselves and position ourselves to become experts and get all the education we can attain.

I often reflect on the sacrifice my parents made to help us have a better life. Our early beginnings were humbling. My father grew up in Sedalia, North Carolina, and he had to drop out of school in the sixth grade to help support the family; at the age of twelve, he was tragically injured. My dad was kicked in the head by a mule and lost his hearing. My father had to learn a new way of communicating through sign language. What was amazing about my father was his ability to communicate with people, despite being hearing impaired.

My father was loyal and dedicated to his employer, working hard for the same company for forty years. The name of the business was Banner Trulove; it was a trucking and food distribution company. My father died of cancer, in 1990, at the age of seventy-one. My father had many friends of all ethnic backgrounds, and hundreds attended his funeral. When my mother retired from Moses Cone Hospital, she had spent most of her days walking and was in excellent shape. She was a diligent and hard worker.

My father and mother took us to church and wanted us to know God. What stands out to me about my parents is their love for people and how they were always helping others. The principles I learned from my parents were the value of hard work, being on time, and being early for appointments. Even though my dad had a temper, he also had a humorous side to him that would lift the tension.

When families understand the history of their heritage, they can be better equipped to fulfill their purpose and function better as people. When families follow their convictions and principles and do not compromise those principles, they help their families stay safe and secure. Parents must have a vision and pass that vision on to their children. Vision means asking, "Where are we going?" and then showing them the details of how to get there.

We must learn to cooperate with the Holy Spirit in charting the course God intends for us. When we are not seeking the heart of God, we can easily veer off course and end up in a place we will regret. God has dreams and visions for our lives, and we must ask God for His guidance to fulfill the plans He has place on life.

In his *Book of Prophecies,* Christopher Columbus stated, "God gave me the spirit and the intelligence for the task … It was the Lord who put in my mind (I could feel His hand upon me) to sail to the Indies … There is no question that the inspiration was from the Holy Spirit, because he comforted me with rays of marvelous illumination from the Holy Scriptures." God desires to lead us and hopes we will glorify Him and fulfill His intended purpose.

We must work toward God's purpose, share God's love with people, and win people to Jesus Christ—despite living this life with all the challenges that come our way. Actions speak louder than words, but our words must be communicated clearly so people can hear what we are all about. Our words must match our actions so people are not confused. We communicate in three ways: words, tone, and body language.

Parents are to let their children know that they are valued and loved. We must train and teach principles from the Bible that help them form their philosophies, their identities, and their belief systems.

I am learning to stay calm when everything seems out of my control, and I am learning to stay collected when I want to quickly respond and try to fix a problem. I am learning to operate and live opposite to the ways I have lived for most of my life.

When we believe what God says about us, our whole picture and purpose in life changes for the better. Gideon was called a mighty man of God, and he questioned God when He revealed his identity. Gideon wanted proof of his purpose and identity by asking for signs. Gideon activated his faith in God and prepared an offering in the form of making bread for God. And when Gideon asked for confirmation, he learned to cooperate and listen to God's specific instructions.

We must consistently learn to grow and elevate in Christ Jesus. We are to be students of the kingdom for our entire lives. We must learn the art of listening so that we can be ready to speak His Word, His will, and His way into situations that help set people free.

We must realize that there are people who desire for us to quit what we are called to do. We need to learn to maintain our cool in situations where people are intentionally testing us to act out of character. Family members should not try to test boundaries with one another, but they may still try to push you, especially during moments when you are most heated.

Staying calm is imperative when people push every button to upset you.

There are hidden rules in every sphere that indicate if people will support you and stand with you. Also, influencers in a city can make decisions that make things happen for you; they can also choose to make things difficult and block you. In life, we must be careful about what we say in private and in public. We must be on the same page with ourselves and with God so that we are the same leader in private and in public.

When my brother started in his career as an electrician, he was put in multiple situations that would normally cause a person to quit. He was put through a gauntlet of problems, was put in the lowest-quality conditions, and was given helpers who were not competent in the field so that he would fail. He was looked down upon and given the worst job assignments, and his counterparts were given the best jobs. However, he was determined and stayed the course—and he did the best he could in difficult situations. He became an excellent electrician, and he was sent on jobs all around the city as a troubleshooter, finding problems where others had difficulties. He was respected and relied on as one of the most qualified electricians in the region.

We must learn the art of endurance:

> Endure suffering along with me as a good
> soldier of Christ Jesus. (2 Timothy 2:3 NLT)

Trials and trouble forge leaders toward greatness. Jeremiah 1:5 (NLT) tells us that God knew you before you were born and designed you with specific skills and gifts to be a certain kind of leader. There are things that only you can do; therefore, the world needs what is in you to make the world a better place.

Jesus told him, "I am the way, the truth,
and the life. No one can come to the Father
except through me." (John 14:6 NLT)

How you think about life and yourself affects everything
you do. The truth sets you free from error and lies that have
held you in bondage.

He learned obedience through the things He
suffered. (Hebrews 5:8 NLT)

Jesus submitted himself fully to the human experience
and obeyed His parents (Luke 2:52 NLT). He lived holy and
fulfilled the will of God. I have lived through the school of
hard knocks and have learned the importance of obedience
to God. I have felt the awful consequences of disobedience. I
have discovered listening to God makes life's outcomes much
smoother. I love teaching young people to help them avoid the
painful consequences of poor decisions. For years, I have said,
"Decisions determine destiny."

We must remember the hall of fame leaders of the Bible.
They all had something in common. They made it a practice of
inquiring of the Lord. David defeated Goliath; Esther saved a
nation; Nehemiah rebuilt the walls of Jerusalem; Peter and the
apostles laid the foundation of the faith through Jesus Christ;
Abraham was the father of humanity; Moses was the deliverer;
and Daniel was the man who excelled in Babylonian empires
through prayer and listening.

God knows everything about you, why you exist, and what
He specifically has in mind for you to do as a leader. Everyone
can be a leader in their specific area of functionality. A car has
forty thousand parts, and every part is vital to operate and
move the vehicle. We must learn what God wants from us so

we can lead others to the place God is going. Sadly, too many leaders do not have God's vision. Consequently, they are blind to God's Word, will, and way. They will lead themselves and those who follow them into a ditch.

> So ignore them. They are blind guides leading the blind, and if one blind person guides another, they will both fall into a ditch. (Matthew 15:14 NLT)

It is imperative that we keep on inquiring of God so that we have the insight to lead ourselves and others to the light in Christ Jesus and help people walk out their faith with wisdom and victory.

We must learn to invite God's kingdom into every area of our lives. We must learn to stay connected to the Rock so that we can withstand the currents of wickedness and the cultural influences that try to drag us away from God's Word, will, and way. We must study and learn what it means to fear God—a holy reverence that comes as we spend time in the scriptures and seek God's presence. It is a process.

As we learn more about God, we will be more in awe of His amazing ways. God is a consuming fire.

> Summon the people before me, and I will personally instruct them. Then they will learn to fear me as long as they live, and they will teach their children to fear me also. (Deuteronomy 4:10 NLT)

Fear is a deep respect that leads to full surrender to God. As we learn to develop reverence, obedience, and friendship with God, we gain understanding of the powerful covenant we have in God.

> Since we are receiving a kingdom that is unshakable, let us be thankful and please God by worshipping Him with holy fear and awe. For our God is a devouring fire (consuming fire). (Hebrews 12:28–29 NLT)

God's kingdom is unshakable; therefore, it is imperative to learn of God's kingdom so that we as servants remain firm and stable in a shaky world and so that our marriages and families remain solid and sound in Christ.

We must learn to stay connected to the people who see our potential.

When I was in tenth grade, after looking at my grades, my coach said, "Rex, you are smart!"

I said, "I am?" No one had ever said that to me before.

The familiar situation reminds me of what God said to Gideon, in Judges 6:12: "You mighty man of valor" (NKJV).

We must allow God through His Word to show us who we really are: kings and priests who are chosen, anointed, and appointed by God. Remember, we are in a battle.

> There is a wide-open door for a great work here, although many oppose me. (Corinthians 16:9 NLT)

Enter that door God has chosen for you and advance the kingdom of God with the force of faith. We must know and learn how our adversary operates using deception, fear, slander, discouragement, and anything that will prevent you from fulfilling God's plan and purpose.

Learning, studying, and knowing the Word of God gives us discernment to the tactics of our enemy. We must constantly train ourselves in the Word of God. You may be asking, "Why?" When we answer and obey God's call, we literally have a bounty on our lives from the kingdom of darkness.

Continuous study and training keep us alert and prepared for the daily battles and schemes the enemy tries to use against us.

> For someone who lives on milk is still an infant and doesn't know how to do what is right. Solid food is for those who are mature, who through training have the skill to recognize the difference between right and wrong. (Hebrews 5:13–14 NLT)

We must desire the meat of the Word so that we can handle life with maturity and skill.

> The godly may trip seven times, but they will get back up. (Proverbs 24:16 NLT)

My greatest mistakes and fleshly fits of rage happened when I bypassed rest. During the times I was fatigued and frustrated, I said things I regret. We must understand human nature. Jesus knows a man's heart is inclined to be deceitful (John 2:23–25 NLT). We cannot put our faith in man or princes—but only in God. We can hope and believe for the best in every person and hope we are all striving to follow Micah 6:8: to do what is right, to love mercy, and walk humbly with God." (NLT)

To be true effective servants of God, we must recognize Satan's modus operandi. We must sharpen our spiritual senses so that we can clearly see and discern when he is in operation. First, we must remember we are not to put our sole trust in men or princes. Man's very nature is fickle, and we are prone to sin because of our sin nature. As we take a close look at our own hearts, we can be double-minded, on an emotional roller coaster, and changing our passions and dreams based on life's circumstances. Unfortunately, we are apt to go astray. Therefore, it is imperative to maintain daily and consistent time spent with Jesus. It keeps on grounded and secure in Him. We must keep our eyes and focus on Jesus. He never fails us, and He continues to build in us solid character-building skills so that we finish strong in life. As long as sin is lurking, Satan is working, and temptation is around, disappointments are bound to happen. God forbid that we disqualify ourselves and pray that God preserves and protects us from evil in Jesus's name.

We must learn to build our lives and family the biblical way:

> A house is built through wisdom and becomes strong through good sense. (Proverbs 24:3 NLT)

We need God's wisdom in leading our families so that we are established on a legacy of unshakable principles that last for generations. One must desire to come to know and grow in Christ and do what He is telling you to do. As you pursue learning and growing, allow God to indelibly etch into your memory His amazing wisdom and knowledge. In Matthew 11:30, Jesus said, "For My yoke is easy and My burden is light" (NLT).

When we are yoked with Jesus, we become determined and disciplined to follow His way of doing things. When we do things God's way, we will see His way is always the best and right way of living. A yoke is a wooden crosspiece that is fastened over the necks of two animals and attached to a plow or cart they are to pull. We naturally want to pull things with our own strength, but when we pull with Jesus, we can focus and clearly fulfill the purpose He intends for us. He knows everything about us and helps us stay the course of plowing, pursuing His will, helping people, and fulfilling the plans and purpose He desires for us.

Knowledge gives us understanding and the ability to make sound decisions, and it helps us be informed of what is truth.

As we learn in Nehemiah 6:1–9 (NLT), we must continue advancing God's work because Satan's agents will attempt to use deception, distraction, and delays in the hope we will stop the work and quit. We must continue pressing forward with God's great work. No matter what rumors or reports come up against us, we must stay the course until the work is finished. We work through discouragement that is brought on by lies. We should not allow anyone to intimidate us and prevent us from completing and continuing the work God has assigned to us.

As leaders and teachers, we must do our part in understanding how to best deliver important truths that make learning exciting and appealing.

> The tongue of the wise makes knowledge appealing, but the mouth of a fool belches out foolishness. (Proverbs 15:2 NLT)

We have a responsibility to study and prepare ourselves to have something to say that will bring hope, life, and purpose. We cannot allow bad habits or bad words be spoken into the minds of aspiring hungry people.

> Intelligent people are always ready to learn.
> Their ears are open for knowledge. (Proverbs
> 18:15 NLT)

As leaders, we must understand that people remember 10 percent of what they read, 20 percent of what they see, 30 percent of what they hear, and 70 percent of what they see and hear at the same time.

> I pray that your love will overflow more and
> more, and that you will keep on growing in
> knowledge and understanding. For, I want
> you to understand what really matters, so
> that you may live pure and blameless lives
> until the day of Christ's return. (Philippians
> 1:9–10 NLT)

Seven Points of Learning

1. Listening helps you discern.
2. Looking alerts you to danger.
3. Liking people helps you understand people.
4. Leadership makes a difference in the lives of people.
5. Language in your body speaks volumes more than words.
6. Life lessons are excellent teachers.
7. Literacy and learning go hand in hand.

Seven enemy tactics that must be discerned!

1. Deception is defined as the action of deceiving someone.
2. Persistence is defined as firm continuance in a course of action despite opposition Nehemiah 6:3–4 (NLT).

3. Slander and gossip are defined as the action or crime of making a false spoken statement that damages a person's reputation. Nehemiah 6:5–9 (NLT) is meant to discourage, get you out of focus, divide, confront, and slander. Instead, tell the truth, trust God, and live above reproach.

4. Avoid infiltration through false teaching (Nehemiah 6:10–14 NLT). There are ways to deal with lies and align with God's Word (1 Timothy 4:1–2 NLT). Know who you are in Christ and avoid infiltration through compromise (1 Corinthians 5:6 NLT). Compromise hinders intimacy with God (Psalm 1:1 NLT).

5. Psychological warfare is defined as actions intended to reduce an opponent's morale (Nehemiah 6:12–19 NLT).

6. Fear is an unpleasant emotion caused by the belief that someone or something is dangerous, likely to cause pain, or a threat. Fear can prevent believers from doing God's work (2 Timothy 1:7 NLT). Pray (Philippians 4:6–7 NLT).

7. An attack is an aggressive and violent action against a person or place. Attacks typically come immediately after victory (Nehemiah 6:15–19 NLT).

Advancing God's work will ensure the enemy will look for ways to bring you down. Greater is He who is in you than he who is in the world.

> You have already won a victory over those people, because the spirit who lives in you is greater than the spirit who lives in the world.
> (1 John 4:4 NLT)

Elevate Questions

1. Why should we be hungry to learn?
2. What did you learn from this chapter?
3. Why should we learn from every circumstance and trial?
4. How do learning and obedience go hand in hand?
5. Why must we learn the will of God and follow His will for our lives?
6. Why must we learn to discern and understand human propensities?
7. What did Jesus mean when he said His yoke is easy?

Prayers to Pray over Yourself and Your Family

1. "We pray that love would overflow more and more from you Lord into us and that we keep growing and in knowledge and understanding in Jesus's name" (Philippians 1:9–10 NLT).
2. "Father, help us develop our intelligence by embracing your word in Jesus's name" (Proverbs 18:15 NLT).
3. "Father, help us develop our knowledge and to impart what we learn with creativity that will cause a thirst and hunger in people for your Word in Jesus's name" (Proverbs 15:2 NLT).
4. "Father, help us endure suffering and persecution as soldiers and keep our focus on your agenda in Jesus's name" (2 Timothy 2:3 NLT).
5. "Father, we thank you for training your people to be warriors, how to use our spiritual weapons and earthly hands to advance your kingdom in Jesus's name" (Psalm 144:1 NLT).

6. "Father, help us be diligent and consistent in seeking you first and foremost in all matters and decisions in Jesus's name" (Matthew 6:33 NLT).

7. "Father, help us seek you fervently by studying the scriptures faithfully and daily in Jesus's name" (John 5:39 NLT).

——— EFFORT ———

GIVING YOUR ABSOLUTE BEST

Now is the time we put into action what we have learned and put feet to the vision. God has a plan, a strategy, and a vision that must be implemented. It has four letters and is called *work*. Effort and work go hand in hand, and planning with detail and hard work leads to production and profit.

I worked on my uncle's ranch during high school; it was intense working from sunup to sundown during the summer. We were loading bales of hay, moving rocks, shoveling dirt, and handling whatever was needed to complete the job. The same kind of effort is required in sports, which requires intense work all year round, including wind sprints, jogging long distances, lifting weights, studying, and team building. To elevate, you must take 100 percent responsibility for your life to get the best results. From there, you will learn to clarify your life purpose, your vision, and what you genuinely want.

What is effort? It is giving your absolute best—everything you have—and expending every ounce of strength, energy, and enthusiasm into a task. Hard work positions you and molds you into a leader.

> Work hard and become a leader; be lazy and become a slave. (Proverbs 12:24 NLT)

Laziness hurts you and is not productive toward fulfilling what you were designed to do.

> A lazy person is as bad as someone who destroys things. (Proverbs 18:9 NLT)

Are you working hard? Are you giving your best? Hard work and endeavoring to do your work with excellence position you to elevate. Hard work gives us a sense of significance and accomplishment.

> Good planning and hard work leads to prosperity, but hasty shortcuts lead to poverty. (Proverbs 21:5 NLT).

There is one way of fulfilling your divine purpose and destiny, and it is called working for it. Our prayer should be this: "Lord, show me the areas that need my undivided attention to elevate to the place you desire for me to be—in Jesus's name."

Effort also means using physical or mental energy to do something, exerting great effort to achieve victory. Elevating requires the work of an ox, which is a daily discipline. In *The Success Principles*, Jack Canfield said, "Most people are conditioned to blame something outside of themselves for the parts of their life they don't like. We blame parents, bosses, our friends, the media, weather, the economy, lack of money or anything we can pin the blame on."

Leadership is action. We must be going and growing in Christ every day, giving our best in every endeavor.

> For the people had worked with enthusiasm.
> (Nehemiah 4:6 NLT)

We must put our best effort, energy, and enthusiasm into our devotion to God and what He has assigned us to do.

I want to share some insights from the life of a football player and what goes on in the thinking of the running back position. I played this position in high school and four years of college—playing my first collegiate game against Boston College—and I learned and was coached up a lot. The first and foremost responsibility of running backs is to be an excellent listener and to pay attention to the specifically designed plays since they are to be executed with excellent timing and precision. Secondly, everyone's assignment is vital to the success of the entire team. Running backs must block, be decoys, run the football, run passing routes, and do much more. Regardless of the role, every responsibility must be executed with great effort.

Running backs must be quick and fast and look for openings and daylight when running the football. This is especially true when eleven defenders are trying to knock you out and stop you from gaining ground to advance the offense and to keep you from first downs and touchdowns. Running backs must outsmart the defense, outsprint the defense, outplay the defense, out-hustle the defense, out-endure the defense, and outrun the defense to the end zone. Running backs must brace themselves to be hit on every play.

In all my years of playing football, the worst hits, I ever experienced were the ones I did not see coming. My first hit of that sort was in Tennessee. I took the handoff from the quarterback and went to the right side. I saw the hole opening and the beautiful green grass in the end zone. Like other times, I began to turn on my 4.2 speed, lifted my chest, and started my sprint to the end zone. Suddenly, I saw nothing. The hit was so hard from the defender that I was immediately stopped. I felt like I had been hit by a truck and was knocked back several yards. My teammates had to help me up, my chest and sternum were badly hurt, and my shoulder pads were busted. I ended up being sidelined for the remainder of the game with a fractured sternum. I had to brace my chest on the bus all the way back to North Carolina.

Another responsibility of running backs is being a decoy; running backs cannot give any hint of the direction their play is going. Defensive players do a lot to study the tendencies of offenses and the players. Running backs must line up and get in the same stance on every play to not give away what the next play will be. Linebackers will watch how a running back reacts or responds on running plays and pass plays. The body language and acting ability must be on an Academy Award level.

For running backs, so much effort is required to be good. You need to be studying film of defenses, looking over scouting reports of players, learning the type of defense you are going against, and preparing for the tendencies of linebackers to stunt or blitz on specific downs. There are so many plays that must be memorized, and adjustments need to be made to certain types of defenses.

> Give your complete attention to these matters. Throw yourself into your tasks so that everyone will see your progress. (1 Timothy 4:15 NLT)

When you have put the time and effort into the endeavor God has assigned to you, people become intrigued and want to know more about who you are as a person. Because of the public position we have, we must be of a humble spirit and a servant attitude to offer help and encouragement to people. Developing people skills helps you in all your relationships now and in the future.

A healthy marriage relationship also requires hard work and intentional effort. In a marriage relationship, there must be a humble and servant attitude. Both husband and wife must put their absolute best efforts into cultivating a friendship and companionship, which will enhance their relationship.

Training your children in the precepts of God also takes hard work.

> But watch out! Be careful never to forget what you yourself have seen. Do not let these memories escape from your mind as long as you live! And be sure to pass them on to your children and grandchildren. (Deuteronomy 4:9 NLT)

This is a clear mandate from God to parents. We have one life to live, and we must give the best because in the end, we don't want regrets for not doing our best. I attended a conference called "Revamp," and one of the speakers challenged us all to "step up, step in, and step out into our destinies." Are you stepping up to the challenge of fulfilling your purpose? Are you stepping into God's plan through spending time with the Father? And are you stepping out into what He has chosen you to do in your lifetime?

Life can hit you like a ton of bricks, and there will be days when you will feel like giving up. Life is woven together of good and not so good experiences, but in time, a beautiful tapestry is created that allows the grace of God to flow in our lives through challenges and victories. We must continue to reach out for kairos moments by giving our best efforts.

Time accelerates, and studies show how people feel when they are facing the end of their lives. Some people may not fear death, but they wonder if they have fulfilled all that they were supposed to do during their lifetimes. David fulfilled his purpose and went to sleep. Another rude awakening is that too many individuals are sleeping while God is trying to lead them. They are wasting their precious time, which should be used to help serve and build up God's people. We must be about our Father's business building His kingdom.

Sound the alarm! It is time to wake up from our stupor and laziness; we need to get about our Father's business. What impossible task has God called you to do? Gideon defeated thousands with just three hundred warriors who aligned with God's strategy.

> From the days of John the Immerser until now the kingdom of the Heavens is taken by violence, and shares in the Heavenly kingdom are sought with the most ardent zeal and the most intense exertion and violent men are seizing it, each one claiming eagerly for himself. (Matthew 11:12 One New Man Bible)

This verse clearly explains that we are in a war, and we must put everything we can into advancing God's kingdom because opposing forces are trying to prevent that and destroy us. The kingdom is simply bringing God's order and authority to your home, community, city, county, state, and country.

Kingdom in Greek is *Basileia*, which means royal power, kingship, dominion, and rule. God commands us to bring His governing authority, royal power, and dominion into the earth realm so that we can rule according to God's Word, will, and way. Everyone has the responsibility to seek God for themselves so that they can experience God and the victory that comes from pursuing and seeking God.

The word violence is *biazo* in Greek, which means to use force, apply force, ardent zeal and to press forward for the glory of God. In sports, a team can have all the winning ingredients—the talent, skills, and tools to succeed—but they must act on it to achieve victory. It will not be handed to them, and in the kingdom of God, He has given us the resources necessary for victory. However, we must use every ounce of zeal, energy, effort, and enthusiasm to gain that victory.

We must do our part just as Gideon did in Judges 6 (NLT). Gideon was given the game plan from God, but Gideon first had to use all the skills he had. When he did all he could by sticking out his neck and risking his life, God showed up on his behalf. Gideon used everything he had, and God multiplied his efforts.

Personal Note: The ability to run a 4.2 second forty-yard dash and the ability to run a four hundred-meter relay split in 47.1 seconds did not happen by sitting on my behind. This ability came with hours, weeks, and years of training. I had no idea that I had that kind of speed and ability. God knew, and we must give our very best in every endeavor He assigns to us so that we can be used by God with maximum ability.

A violent man in the Greek is *Biastés*, which means energetic, and those who strive to obtain its privileges with the utmost eagerness and effort. The word *take* is *Harpazo*—another Greek word that means to seize, carry off by force, to snatch, or claim for oneself. I have coined the phrase "You have a destiny," but you must go and seize your destiny. You must go and take it and claim it as yours. There should be no more holding back. Go for it—you have nothing to lose. It is your time to elevate for the glory of God and snatch your divine destiny with force in Jesus's name!

What is your greatest fear?

> What I always feared has happened to me.
> What I dreaded has come true. (Job 3:25 NLT)

We often do not give our best efforts because we fear the future. We allow past mistakes and failures to stop us from pursuing God's best for our lives. We must go and obtain what God has assigned to our lives. The children of Israel were promised many blessings, but they had to fight for those promises. They had to renounce fear and start believing God by faith, knowing He would deliver them. When they stepped up, God showed up on their behalf.

Because of my lack of knowledge in raising my children, I displayed much anger toward them. I cannot tell you the countless number of overreactions I had to my children. I have recognized that I was afraid, which was a generational curse that I had, and I needed to keep it broken off between my children and me. I came to a place where I had to literally place my children and family in God's hands and trust God to protect and care for them.

Parents have a huge responsibility to be vigilant and discerning about the well-being of our children. We have parental roles and a responsibility to be intentional in teaching and training our children to know right from wrong, to be kind and loving to others, and to know how to recognize unacceptable behavior. To truly help our loved ones, we must develop the art of hearing the voice of God. We must learn to encourage our families, help them live well by spending time together, and point them to the source of life: Jesus. We must HELP them (hear, encourage, live, and point).

We have a responsibility to put effort into planning for the future. If we truly value our loved ones, we will think ahead and ensure provision is there for future generations.

> But those who won't care for their relatives, especially those in their own household, have denied the true faith. Such people are worse than unbelievers. (1 Timothy 5:8 NLT)

This verse tells us we must be prayerful and that we must plan, produce, provide for our families, and fulfill our divine purpose. *Provide* is from the Greek word *pronoeo*, meaning foresee, think, look beforehand, care for, and consider in advance, and perceive. Real value for our loved ones is being there for them with physical affection, emotional support, spiritual leadership, financial support to meet their basic needs, love and acceptance, and shelter. Maslow's hierarchy of needs theory includes physiological needs, safety needs, love and belonging, esteem, and self-actualization.

Seven points of our absolute best.
1. Eager to grow and become better.
2. Eagle character: To mount up to new heights.
3. Earnest intention to work in your calling and passion.
4. Economic wisdom to that helps transform lives.
5. Educate to emancipate from destructive thinking.
6. Essential tools utilized to help others succeed.
7. Eternity hangs in the balance: We must tell others the truth about life and death.

Elevate Questions
1. Are you dependable enough to carry out projects to completion?

2. What goes on in the mind of a running back?
3. Do you believe we should view marriage as work?
4. What does "the kingdom of heaven suffers violence" mean (Matthew 11:12)?
5. Is there any fear that you have not dealt with or faced?
6. Why is it important to place our children in God's hands?
7. What does the acronym HELP mean?

Prayers to Pray over Yourself

1. Father, help me put the necessary energy, enthusiasm, and effort into the endeavors You have called me to lead in Jesus's name (Proverbs 12:24 NLT).
2. Father, help me prayerfully plan according to Your will and design in Jesus's name (Proverbs 21:5 NLT).
3. Father, help me be strong and courageous, resisting fear and discouragement, for You are with me in Jesus's name (Joshua 1:9 NLT).
4. Father, help us daily have the mind and will to work in building Your kingdom in Jesus's name (Nehemiah 4:6 NLT).
5. Father, help me give complete attention and give very my best effort into the task assigned to us in Jesus's name (1 Timothy 4:15 NLT).
6. Father, help us hold Your truths and principles high in our lives and not forget Your Word, will, and way. Help us impart these truths to our children and grandchildren in Jesus's name (Deuteronomy 4:9 NLT).
7. Father, with Your power and authority, help us advance your kingdom and preach Your Word, uncompromising in Jesus's name (Matthew 11:12 NLT).

VALUE

THE VALUE OF TIME

Value: the regard that something is held to deserve; the importance, worth, or usefulness of something.

We learn what God values by learning what He hates. God dislikes behavior that is warped and is not being used for its intended purpose. God created us to walk in humility, which enables us to recognize that we are nothing without Him. God gives us the ability to have life—and to live life to the utmost.

God gave us the gift of life, and to destroy precious life is to throw away His beautiful, unique masterpiece. If you spend your energy planning evil, you are wasting your creative ideas, which will be counted worthless in the end. They will instead be burned and cast into the abyss with the devil and his demons.

God dislikes the actions of those who intentionally spread lies that hurt and harm precious, innocent minds for the purpose of power and control. God detests those who sow seeds of division because God knows the power of unity and desires to bless beyond measure, and those who sow discord will one day stand before God.

God hates pride; therefore, we must develop humility. God hates lying tongues; therefore, we must walk in truth. Since

God hates hands that shed innocent blood, we must protect innocent lives. God hates hearts that devise wicked plans, feet that are swift in running to evil, false witnesses who speak lies, and those who sow discord among their brethren. God detest these ways because these attitudes have caused much heartache and problems for humankind, and these attitudes are sinful. We must endeavor to keep the unity of the Holy Spirit by recognizing these sinful attitudes and confront them when they try to arise.

> There are six things the Lord hates—no, seven things he detests: haughty eyes, a lying tongue, hands that kill the innocent, a heart that plots evil, feet that race to do wrong, a false witness who pours out lies, a person who sows discord in a family. (Proverbs 6:16–19 NLT)

> I love those who love Me. Those who search will find me. (Proverbs 8:17 NLT)

When we value who God is and are intentional about spending time with Him, we will develop a special affection for God. We will see life in the light of eternity. We will see true value in building God's kingdom and being His holy instrument in the Master's hand.

When I was able to work and serve with the Billy Graham Evangelistic Association, it was such an honor. Dr. Billy Graham was a man who greatly valued the Word of God; he dedicated his life to preaching the Gospel to millions of people for seven decades. The word that describes his work is amazing—how the Lord prepared Dr. Billy Graham for His work on every continent in the world.

Another amazing glimpse I had was meeting Dr. Billy Graham's grandson, Will Graham. Will and I were both preaching at the annual conference of the Christian Meeting and Conventions Association (CMCA) in Roanoke, Virginia, in 2018. I was the opening guest speaker, and Will Graham was the closing speaker. It was a humbling experience to be on the same platform with a member of the Graham family.

A fascinating moment occurred on the evening Will Graham was speaking. I went up to introduce myself, and as I approached him and stated who I was, he said, "I know who you are, and I want to thank you for extending the ministry of my grandfather." His humility was obviously apparent, and I could sense the mantle of his grandfather, Dr. Billy  Graham. When he preached that evening, I could hear the sound bites of his grandfather. Through Will Graham, I received a glimpse of the humility and the love for people that his grandfather showed throughout his lifetime.

A healthy home is where parents govern there home according to biblical standards of love, respect, and regard for one another. It is also where husband and wife submit to God's Word and one another out of reverence for God. Families who practice godliness in private and walk out their faith daily leave a mark of success with their loved ones. This is how families pass down their values for generations.

Therefore, it is imperative that family members live and share their faith stories with their families; this gives them the ability to communicate, and the stories teach children how to work through life's problems.

Families must have times of bonding to build strong and healthy relationships. When families have bonding times, they can build lasting relationships. Bonding requires time, listening, and understanding, and it gives you the freedom to share your dreams and aspirations. Home is where loving memories are created. Sharing stories helps children develop healthy memories as they navigate through life's challenges.

We must believe for the best and be encouraging to our families in every season and stage of life. Unfortunately, many families experience dysfunction because they have not learned the art of communicating and will not even attempt to communicate. Therefore, the younger generation is unable to deal with their problems in a healthy manner. You will never grow beyond the ability to hear and receive pleasant or unpleasant truths. The family is the place to share one's true heart by learning to confront one's problems with grace and humility.

Pride in relationships is destructive; therefore, always avoid prideful behavior. Pride will not take responsibility for wrongful actions. Prideful people refuse to listen and understand the root of the matter.

> An open rebuke is better than hidden love.
> Wounds from a sincere friend are better
> than many kisses from an enemy. (Proverbs
> 27:5–6 NLT)

These verses clearly show us that if we really love our children and friends, we must tell the truth. The truth does not always feel good, but the truth is necessary for us to grow and be healthy citizens.

A man should ask his wife and family what they see that could hinder his leadership ability. And the wife should ask the same question. Men must be wise and gentle in their responses because you do not want to be in the doghouse. Instead, speak the truth with loving kindness. I cannot tell you how many times I have spoken truth without care, concern, or caution.

When we share truth with humility and grace, the medicine of truth is received better. One of the reasons conflicts are never resolved in families is that the members simply will not listen to each other.

> Understand this, my dear brothers and sisters:
> You must all be quick to listen, slow to speak,
> and slow to get angry. (James 1:19 NLT)

Healthy families choose to follow God's Word to keep order instead of chaos, develop mutual respect versus disrespect, and exercise the authority given by God versus no authority. God places high regard on the marriage between a man and a woman:

> The man who finds a wife finds a treasure,
> and he receives favor from the Lord. (Proverbs
> 18:22 NLT)

I studied this in the Hebrew text, and this what I discovered. If you catch a female, you will acquire benefits that furnish success and satisfaction from the one and only supreme God. When a man finds a wife, he is walking with his wife in God's divine order and blessing. A wife who seeks God is affectionate, compliments her husband, nurtures the children, takes care of her household, and is frugal. One must clearly recognize you are blessed to have a woman of this caliber. We must acknowledge and value all the sacrifices that our spouses make.

I have a story about taco salad. I had asked my family to move back to North Carolina from Colorado, which meant my wife would need to drive 1,700 miles in a fifteen-passenger van and trailer, find a place to live in a specific district, and get our children registered for school. All of this happened while I was finishing up camps in Texas and Oklahoma because I had made a commitment to these camps prior to knowing we would be moving at the same time.

On a beautiful fall day, we were sitting around the dinner table and having a discussion. Our son was on my right, our daughter was on my left, and my wife was sitting directly across from me. I do not remember our conversation that led up to me saying to my wife, "You need to submit!"

Her look was of amazement and alarm at the audacity of my statement. As she got up to leave the table, my wife's plate of chips, beef, beans, lettuce, salsa, hot sauce, dressings, and cheese was lifted into the air and flew across the table— seemingly in slow motion. The plate landed nicely on my side of the table, and all the food was on me! My wife had no idea what had happened because she had exited the kitchen. I looked at my son and daughter and said, "I messed up!" I realized I should not have said what I uttered because of the sacrifices my wife made to get us all moved to North Carolina. I sat there and ate my taco salad with all the food layered upon me. Men, you must watch what you say, especially if your wife has worked hard to help the family meet their goals. Men, let's stop putting our feet in our mouths and think before we speak.

When two people come together in holy matrimony, they reflect God's covenant plan for their family:

> A wise woman builds her home, but a foolish
> woman tears it down with her own hands.
> (Proverbs 14:1 NLT)

A wife who is wise will know how to build up her children and husband so that their home is conducive to learning, and they will become healthy and successful. I am thankful that my wife and I made the commitment for her to be a stay-at-home mom during our children's impressionable years. It was a huge sacrifice to live on one income, but it was worth it. I believe every family must pray and plan how they want to raise their children and decide who will help nurture them as they grow up.

The value of prayer is imperative in keeping a family together. The story of the ten virgins is a prime example of what happens to individuals and families when they are prayerless and not digging into the Holy Scriptures daily. In Matthew 25:1–12 (NLT), Jesus shares the story of the wise and foolish virgins. This text describes the importance of spiritual preparedness of five who were prepared and five who were not spiritually prepared. The five who were prepared represent how we must daily be filled with God's Word, study to show we approve, be filled with the Holy Spirit, and abide daily in God's awesome presence. In God's presence is where we find the oil of gladness.

The unprepared five virgins symbolize the opposite. They were not in God's Word, did not heed the whispers and prompts from the Holy Spirit, and were not pursuing God's presence through worship. Spiritual preparedness is an individual responsibility. The text also reveals that we cannot properly help others if we are not properly filled with oil that comes from God, which equips us to be spiritually prepared and pour it into others. Living victoriously requires understanding time and timing. When we understand time and how we spend time with the One who is outside of time and who created time, it helps us value the time endowed to us. We have 86,400 seconds in a day and 168 hours in a week. We must make the most of the time we have by waking early to pray, plan, and prepare for our days and weeks.

The meaning of the parable is to encourage you to be watchful and prayerful because we do not know the day or hour when our Lord will come for us. Do not slack on your Word and prayer life; it helps you be prepared for the King and helps you be ready at any moment. In this story, the oil symbolizes knowledge of the Word or Torah, which provides spiritual revelation and illumination. Oil is also a symbol of joy and is called the oil of gladness. The principle of this parable is to be spiritually ready and to expect the unexpected.

Communication comes from the Latin word *Communis*, which means common, taking personal time to build a relationship, sharing, and care. The Greek word *Koinoneo* means to share, contribute, and impart. Between 60 and 90 percent of all communication consists of body language, eye contact, facial expressions, and tone rather than words. There are different types of communication: written, verbal, and nonverbal.

We must be Christ-centered, clear, calm, and consistent people who are full of grace. When our communication is delivered with these four fundamental principles, trust can be built. When trust is built, healthy communication lines remain open to understand other points of view.

Unhealthy communication comes in many forms, including silence, sarcasm, cynicism, unpredictable behavior, and lack of transparency. Communication boundaries must be established when yelling and screaming are happening, no one is listening, or people are grasping the root of the problem.

To bring resolve, time must allow for members to cool down. When family members have had time to vent with someone who will listen, then one can go back to seeking harmony and healing from misunderstanding.

For families to succeed, there must be people in their lives who have the spiritual maturity and authority to speak into the situation and circumstances. We have learned the hard way that you do not choose friends as accountability partners who lack spiritual maturity and leadership; immature people cannot be objective to speak truth to all involved. Each family member must make the decision to follow the Ephesians 4:26–27 (NLT) model:

> And don't sin by letting anger betray you. Do not let the sun go down while you are still angry, for anger gives a foothold to the devil.

We must deal with problems and not let them fester and become bitter; we must seek to resolve and get better in our relationships. What if problems are not resolved before nightfall? Pray fervently and ask for God's grace to protect hearts and pray God's grace over the situation.

Satan looks for ways to get his foot into relationship and take over with poisonous feelings and words. We must deal with the pain and hurt and go to God to help us release unforgiveness:

> Get rid of all bitterness rage, anger, harsh words, and slander, as well as all types of evil behavior. Instead, be kind to each other, tenderhearted, forgiving one another, just as God through Christ has forgiven you. (Ephesians 4:31–32 NLT)

The value of God's Word will provide a way to help us provide vision so that our families remain vibrant in all seasons of life. We taught our children the scriptures, and we helped our children memorize verses of the Bible. I helped Christian memorize up to thirty-two verses when he was in elementary school.

> Study this book of instruction continually.
> Meditate on it day and night so you will be
> sure to obey everything written in it. Only
> then will you prosper and succeed in all you
> do. (Joshua 1:8 NLT)

We also provided our children with other resources, which had faith-inspiring messages, such as "Adventures in Odyssey" at bedtime, which is produced by Focus on the Family, and we also watched faith-based films that shared biblical principle of how to solve problems God's way.

> Those who spare the rod of discipline hate
> their children. Those who love their children
> care enough to discipline them. (Proverbs
> 13:24 NLT)

Parents who discipline their children are helping them to function properly in society and understand boundaries and authority. I was a troubled child running through the streets, fighting, stealing, and causing chaos. I also had no desire to attend school or learn.

The sad part about my upbringing is that I cannot remember being spanked by my father. He was hassled by my older brothers when he attempted to discipline them, and they gave my dad a lot of pushback. I still remember when my dad decided he was done disciplining after a confrontation with my brothers. I noticeably recognized that when I was in trouble, he acted as though he did not care anymore—and he did not give me the discipline I needed and deserved. Do I believe my dad loved me? That answer would be yes. I just believe he was tired of fighting for what was the right thing to do, and his spirit was broken by life's challenges.

We were a family that had love and respect for each other. We attended church, and my mom and dad had healthy relations. When we moved to the projects, our family dynamics changed dramatically. Our language included lots of cussing, and there were fights, hatred, sexual activity, and drug use. When I saw what had happened to my family, I made the mistake of over-disciplining my children. I would react instead of responding to my children with unloving discipline. There were times my discipline was harsh and did not fit the infraction. Instead of building respect, I instilled fear. I had no idea that I was reacting out of fear instead of loving discipline. My mistakes started showing up more during their teen years. Many families are experiencing brokenness and hopelessness and have given up on discipline. Parents, don't give up on your children.

I remember looking for balance in those years, and with God's help—and by His grace—He helped us through those years. Our two children respect the Lord and have become productive, hardworking citizens who know right from wrong.

When I reflect on my childhood, I wish my dad had disciplined me when I needed it. I wish my parents had nurtured me more and spent time with me while I sat alone in the hospital for weeks with a large cut on my forehead and a broken femur in traction. The femur is the largest bone in the body. Unfortunately, that moment in time has left an indelible mark upon my life, and just writing about this brings tears to my eyes. I was only seven years old, but I still remember the hospital room, the smell, and the nurses who tended to me. A teacher tried to help me learn, but I refused to cooperate. I remember the little black and white television that took quarters to use every half hour. I remember thinking, *I don't want quarters and television; I want my dad and mom.* I know my dad worked hard, and my mom had no license to drive a car to visit, but it still deeply bothered me.

Despite the crisis, I give God the glory. I can move forward in life simply because I am loved and affirmed by my heavenly Father. He has blessed me beyond what I deserve. I sometimes wonder why God chose me to write about this subject since I am the least qualified for this subject. My role as husband has fallen short many times over the years, and I feel like I failed miserably in my role as a father. I wish I had been a better husband and father. I am just being honest, but I can honestly say I have lived a life of prayer and the study of God's Word before my family. They have clearly witnessed my love for the Father and my commitment to fulfill my purpose and destiny. I have been there to help them succeed to the best of my ability. Both Vickie and I have been integrally involved in our children's academic and extracurricular activities. We were intentionally involved in our children's lives, which is a clear demonstration of how much we care about their success.

We have a responsibility to teach our children biblical values so that each generation helps maintain strong families for generations to come.

> Let each generation tell its children of your
> mighty acts; let them proclaim your power.
> (Psalm 145:4 NLT).

Vickie and I taught our children about God, and they can testify to many of God's amazing interventions and testimonies of amazing power and ability demonstrated in our lives. We must live with integrity, desire to learn the scriptures, and pursue our divine purpose. This will enable our children to maintain a spiritual legacy of blessings and health.

> Fathers, do not provoke your children to anger by the way you treat them. Rather, bring them up with the discipline and instruction that comes from the Lord. (Ephesians 6:4 NLT)

> And you must commit yourselves wholeheartedly to these commands that I am giving you today. Repeat them again and again to your children. Talk about them when you are at home and when you are on the road, when you are going to bed and when you are getting up. (Deuteronomy 6:6–7 NLT)

God places a high value on acts of kindness throughout the Bible. When we are doing good deeds, we can impact people's lives through God's power. These opportunities communicate the love of God and the Gospel and will help transform lives with God's Word. We must regularly serve our neighbors with acts of love—during good times and crisis moments. Remember these four principles: affection, communication, teaching, and serving (ACTS).

We demonstrate to our families and friends what we value by how we spend our time and our money. According to the kingdom, this is how we are to prioritize:

1. God
2. marriage
3. children
4. ministry/work
5. goals, such as home, future, and finances

Doing what we love is the key to enjoying life and being intentional with the things we hold dear. Our values are caught and taught; our children learn our values. Our family valued our vacations. My children still talk about our vacations to Disney World and how they enjoyed staying at the hotel that had a pool, visiting Mount Rushmore, and our vacation to Dillon, Colorado. We played board games, went on hikes, and watched family-centered movies.

Even though we made many mistakes as parents, I am glad we were intentional about spending time with our children. I am glad we read to our children. When we spend time with our children, the time communicates that we love them, and they will value what we value. Actions speak louder to us as humans then words, especially to children.

Devoting ourselves to the strength of our families, we often think they should be free of problems.

> I have told you all this so that you may have peace in me. Here on earth, you will have many trial and sorrows. But take heart because I have overcome the world. (John 16:33 NLT)

There are seasons of trouble that come to families, and how you handle those seasons determines if you will elevate to the next level of growth. During seasons of trouble, it is easy to check out and quit. In a culture where divorce is so prevalent, a husband and wife have more acceptance of leaving their family because the culture tells us we must be happy. We are conditioned to do this by our culture instead of following God's way. Our spouses are not called to make us happy, but to help us become holy—more like Christ Jesus—which requires dying to self. It is a hard pill to swallow for most of us. Mutual respect, honor, forgiving hearts, and acts of kindness must be an ongoing process in every home.

The value of the soul is what is important to God; therefore, it must be important to us. Eternity hangs in the balance, ensuring our loved ones and friends hear the truth of the Gospel—that Jesus died for our sins—and if we repent and ask Jesus into our hearts, we will be saved. I remember enjoying visiting Connelly Springs, North Carolina, to spend time with Vickie's parents. I always felt right at home, and I felt lots of love. Vickie's mom, Myra Hardy, would make a sweet potato pie just for me. I loved the shaded trees and walking through the fields. On one of those special days, I was spending time with Vickie's father in his front yard out in the country of North Carolina; in the distance, we could see the beautiful Blue Ridge Mountains. I would just listen to his stories about life, and then the moment came when I asked him if he would like to receive Jesus as his Lord and Savior. He said, "Yes." I had the amazing honor of leading my father-in-law, Kenneth Hardy, to Christ, and we witnessed a changed man who fell in love with Jesus and his Word, before he departed this green earth at age eighty-nine.

We, as a family, must return to our first love:

> But I have this complaint against you. You don't love me or each other as you did at first. Look how far you have fallen! Turn back to me and do the works you did at first. If

> you do not repent, I will come and remove your lampstand from its place among the churches. (Revelation 2:4–5 NLT)

Return to your commitment to daily prayer and daily Bible study. Return to your commitment to church attendance and serving in your local church or ministry. Return to witnessing to everyone that the Holy Spirit prompts us to share the love of Christ. Our beliefs and behaviors should reveal a vivid view that we value God and live by His virtues first and foremost. If we want to live successfully and finish strong, we must incorporate God's values into every area of our lives.

In 2 Peter 1:3–15, we learn that God has given us everything we need to live a godly life. We must learn to appropriate and stand on God's promises. When we are connected to God's divine ability, we become grounded in faith, excellence, knowledge, self-control, endurance, godliness, and brotherly affection. I call these principles the seven pillars of divine ability. To understand God's divine ability to live this life, take look at the meaning of each pillar.

1. Faith. The Greek word is *Pistis,* meaning certainty at accepting God at His Word. It also means truth, belief, a conviction.
2. Virtue. The Greek word is *Arete,* meaning courage.
3. Knowledge. the Greek word is *Gnosis*, meaning practical wisdom in everyday circumstances.
4. Self-control. The Greek word is *Egkrateia*, which means to take a grip of oneself.
5. Steadfastness. The Greek word is *Hupomone*, which means courageous patience, courageous acceptance of everything that life can do to us.

6. Godliness. The Greek word is *Eusebeia*, meaning religion that serves God and man, reverence for God and people, self-sacrificing to meet practical needs.
7. Brotherly affection. The Greek word is *Philadelphia*, which means claims and demands of a personal relationship are not a nuisance, but a joy.

Seven Points to Build Value

1. Vision points out the path for the family.
2. Valleys help the family build spiritual muscles.
3. Vibrant families reveal God's glory.
4. Values help the family stand strong in tough times.
5. Valiant families are brave amid persecution.
6. Vantage points position the family to be viewed in a proper light.
7. Victorious families know that victory comes through God.

Elevate Questions

1. Where do we get our values?
2. Why is healthy communication necessary for a family?
3. How can values help us provide vision for our families?
4. What are God's values in Proverbs 6:16–19 (NLT)?
5. What happened in the taco salad story?
6. What is unhealthy communication?
7. Why must we ensure that the next generation understands what God values?

Seven Prayers to Build Value

1. Father, help us understand how to live by your values and experience abundant life in Jesus's name (Acts 17:28 NLT).

2. Father, we break every generational curse and choose life in Jesus's name (Deuteronomy 30:19–20 NLT).

3. We clothe ourselves in the whole armor of God so that we can withstand the schemes of the enemy in Jesus's name (Ephesians 6:10–18 NLT).

4. Father, we ask that you help husbands and wives love and respect each other in Jesus's name (James 1:19 NLT).

5. Father, help the family get back to the basics of reading and studying Your Word in Jesus's name (2 Timothy 2:15 NLT).

6. Father, help the children be respectful and grow up in homes filled with love and acceptance in Jesus's name (Ephesians 3:18–19 NLT).

7. Lord, we ask You to heal the wounds of abandonment and abuse and help all family members know they are deeply loved in Jesus's name (Ephesians 4:31–32 NLT).

ALIGN

ALIGNING WITH GOD'S AGENDA

Aligned is defined as a place where things are arranged in a straight line, lined up, put in order, straightened, placed, or positioned to come into precise adjustment or correct relative position. In *Redeeming the Time*, Chuck D. Pierce states, "Attitude is linked with posture and how your attitude manifests is part of your alignment." Posture and attitude are linked with positioning. The concept of alignment is linked with the concept of snapping into place of God's order for the future.

At the age of seven, I was struck by a car. I ran into the street without looking, which resulted in traumatic injuries. I broke my femur and had a large cut on my forehead that required several stitches. I was in the hospital for weeks and was placed in traction to reset my femur. The traction held my bone in place so the bone could be properly realigned. Once my femur was reset, I had to be put in a large body cast that covered my entire leg and wrapped around my torso up to my chest. The cast was very heavy. I was not strong enough to stand up by myself initially, but over time, I got used to standing with crutches.

The same process occurred with my collarbone, which I broke playing football. On a cold December day, I was running at full speed and was spun around, which caused me to lose my balance. I then plunged shoulder first into the hard ground, snapping my collarbone. I had to wear a brace to hold my collarbone in place so the bone could line up and heal. When things are out of line, they cannot function properly. Therefore, God wants order in every area of our lives so that everything functions according to its design. We must cooperate with God and adjust to the things that line up with His will and order.

A train is a great example of alignment. A train takes boxcars through the woods, through the heat of summer, and through blizzard conditions. For the train cars to get through all kinds of conditions, the cars must stay connected to the engine. The same principle applies to the family; if we are to make it through all of life's trials, problems, and crises, we must stay connected to the Lord Jesus Christ.

We must get our houses in order, and that begins with the heads of household—the way God designed things. In the beginning, He created male and female, and he clearly spoke this mandate: to be fruitful and multiply. We must line up our lives with God's Word and align with His government so that our homes will be governed according to biblical principles.

Did you know God has a daily agenda for us? To know God's agenda, we must ask Him and walk according to His Spirit. Those who are led by the Spirit are the children of God (Romans 8:13 NLT). We must be intentional to align every area of our lives spiritually, financially, physically, and mentally, which includes marriage and family. Dr. Henry Cloud said, "The fool tries to adjust the truth, so he does not have to adjust to it."

The wise person accepts the truth and aligns their life with standards of truth and righteousness. As long as they stay connected, they stay aligned. We do not always see how following God's ways will impact the present and future generations. As we align with God's will, we discover our perfect place in the Master's hand. We need to align with a pattern of redemption—with the goal of helping people know and experience living for Jesus.

> Remain in Me, and I will remain in you. For a branch cannot produce fruit if it is severed from the vine, and you cannot be fruitful unless you remain in Me. (John 15:4 NLT)

Truth is truth whether we like it or not, and we must continually align with truth and the revelations God reveals to us. God takes us from glory to glory in His manifested presence—faith to faith, confidence to confidence, or strength to strength—and we become stronger and stronger with every test and trial. As we elevate with the Lord, we must be intentional to stay on the frequency, altitude, and elevation God desires for us.

Luke 5 is an excellent example of the disciples aligning with God's agenda. In Luke 5:1–11 (NLT), Jesus was preaching on the Sea of Galilee. Many were present to hear the oracles coming from Jesus. Jesus noticed two empty boats and asked Simon to push him out in the boat; this allowed the crowd to have a better view.

After Jesus finished teaching, He told Peter to go fish in a deeper area and to let down the nets.

Peter responded that they had fished all night and had not caught one fish, but Peter reluctantly listened to the divine instructions. This time, Peter had the catch of a lifetime. They caught so many fish that the nets were tearing—and the boats were sinking. He quickly called for his fishing partners to help with the large harvest of fish. At that moment, Peter realized he was in the presence of a deity. He fell to his knees and asked Jesus to leave because he was a sinful man. Peter was awestruck by the number of fish.

We can clearly see when Peter lined up with God's instruction and call. Even though he did not understand, God blew his mind with the powerful results of the multitude of fish. The same principle applies to us when we align with God's plan or agenda. Even after several attempts of doing the same thing and failing, don't give up. Keep on pursuing God's plan and purpose, and one day, your obedience plus God's timing will result in exceedingly great things.

I have felt like giving up on ministry many times. I was hoping for a big breakthrough so I could focus solely on ministry. Every time I would go to prayer, the Lord would say, "Stay the course and keep on preaching, teaching, and writing." Obedience is the key with God in every season. No matter how things look, true disciples obey God's commands.

> Can two people walk together without agreeing on the direction? (Amos 3:3 NLT)

To align with God's plan for our lives, we must come into agreement with God's Word, will, wisdom, ways. When we do, we will win. Agreement is powerful when we align our hearts and mouths with God's way. Agreement is the law of the kingdom in being successful and victorious.

Peter's obedience shifted him into alignment with God's divine purpose and destiny.

> If you will obey me, you will have plenty to eat. (Isaiah 1:19 NLT)

Simple obedience to God will open bountiful blessings from God. When you obey God, He will position you for great spiritual blessings that will help you and those around you.

To align means to voice the same conclusion, agree, and confess by aligning your life with His agenda. Bring your life into alignment to the revelation of His word to keep yourself from getting out of flow with God. This is accomplished through daily prayer and study. If you have stepped out of line, bring your behavior into alignment with God's Word. Keep yourself from being self-exalting with a self-inflated ego, which is defined as "edging God out."

> He must increase, and we must decrease.
> (John 3:30 NLT)

We must be full of God instead of self. Pride says, "I did this" or "I built this." It is a self-centered mindset. In our lives, we must understand our purpose and stay on the right path. All men and women must build up their families and fight for their wives, husbands, sons, daughters, and friends.

Nehemiah challenged the leaders to protect their families, homes, and values. If every family cared about truth and accepted this mandate, we could turn the tide of wickedness that has demolished and derailed so many people in our nation. We must rebuild the family values that are gleaned from the Holy Bible. We must get involved in all aspects of society and let our voices be heard.

If you have gotten off course and have crashed with your family and God's values, there is hope and restoration in the cross. When we blunder so badly, God is able to restore our lives.

David repented of his sins, and God forgave him, but there are ramifications for our decisions that impact future generations. Prayers of mercy must be petitioned to God. If God could restore the men and women in the Bible, He can also do it in our lifetimes. He did it for Job, and He will do it for you.

God put Job through a series of tests. Satan said to God, "If you take everything from Job, he will turn away from the faith."

Job stayed in the faith, regardless of losing literally everything. He remained steadfast and faithful to God. Yes, he did question the Lord, but he did not walk away from God. We must align our hearts to faith in God and stop allowing our hearts to be filled with fear:

> What I always feared has happened to me.
> (Job 3:25 NLT)

Discover what your greatest fear is and conquer it in Jesus's name.

Aligning Our Mouths and Hearts with God's Word

In the book of Genesis, God used words to bring things into existence. It is God's will for His servants to utilize this same force and principle. When we align with heaven, we are literally weaponizing our words to shift the atmosphere. Therefore, we must read out loud and pray out loud in Jesus's name. When we share our testimonies, we weaponize them and relive that day when God radically changed and transformed our lives. In the book of Acts, the apostle Paul repeatedly shared his Damascus Road experience.

America's civil law must respect and abide by God's divine law to be fair and accurate in the treatment of people. We must learn God's Word with all our might so that we can be civil in our ways of living, which pleases God. We must write and live our lives for Jesus so that future generations will know that we clearly loved God and marked our love by our actions and writings. We must educate ourselves and develop our knowledge.

We gain knowledge by reading and studying the Holy Scriptures. The fear of the Lord is the beginning of wisdom. In Malachi 2:14–15 (NLT), we learn how serious God is about families. You may wonder why your prayers are not getting results. God sees clearly how we treat our wives. A vow was made to be faithful and loyal to the wife of our youth. God made husband and wife to be one and be blessed. When we are submitted to God, we will bring forth godly seed from this sacred union. Therefore, we must guard our hearts in the form of our wives and families. We must treasure our families and recognize that we are entrusted with a holy responsibility.

We can unpack seven points from this text to help us clearly understand how serious God is about keeping His covenant:

1. Do not be faithless to your wife.
2. Your wife is your companion and ally.
3. We are made one flesh.
4. We have a special bond and spiritual kinship.
5. God desires godly seed from our union.
6. God hates when a man sends away, betrays, or divorces the wife of his youth.
7. We, as sons and daughters, must not allow the devil, the culture, or anyone else to dictate to us to go against God's Word, will, or ways.

We must yield to God's will to honor and glorify our Lord and King. We have been purchased for a high price. Christ's blood paid it all for us to experience abundant life and blessings upon our marriages and families. There are circumstances where a spouse has no control over the circumstances that lead to divorce or the breaking of covenant, but that is where God's amazing grace kicks in. God can take a horrible situation and bring unimaginable redemption.

God is God. He can turn things around for anyone who is willing to completely surrender everything to Him. Many times, we can get out of alignment with God's plan and lose frequency and communication with the Lord. That will drive us into dangerous and destructive territory, which is where the enemy can easily shoot us down. However, when two people are one and choose to align with God and get on the same biblical frequency, they will elevate to new levels of alignment with God, which brings unity and harmony to the marriage and the family.

Too many couples struggle in relationships due to misinformation and being uninformed.

> My people are being destroyed because they
> don't know Me. (Hosea 4:6 NLT)

It would be amazing if we could see how intimidated the devil is when two people come into agreement. The devil knows if he can get two people into pride, bitterness, immorality, and greed, he can get a foothold and start dividing two people who once loved each other deeply. We must understand how Satan's number one agenda is to kill their relationship, steal what they built together to glorify God, and annihilate their life, love, and influence.

The word *divorce* means to divert from the original course, which is Satan's main objective. Satan is always looking for ways to get us away from our divine destinies. Unfortunately, these actions discourage others, and because of that, some people lose hope. The holy covenant they made before God is null and void, which impacts future generations. Hurt and harm goes deep into the memory of loved ones and the unthinkable and unimaginable misery that has happened.

> And you will know the truth, and the truth will set you free. (John 8:32 NLT)

When we understand the truth, we can handle life and our current circumstances with much more grace and understanding. We are free to be ourselves, and we will know life's problems are a part of the journey. We must never give up and never stop pursuing our love in Christ Jesus. The enemy brings chaos and disorder.

> For wherever there is jealousy (Greek word *zelos* meaning an envious, outburst manifestation and contentious rivalry) and selfish ambition (Greek word *eritheia* meaning a desire to put oneself forward, a courting distinction, courting popular applause) there you will find disorder (Greek word *akatastasia* meaning instability, commotion, confusion, and tumult.) and evil (Greek word *phaulos* meaning ethically bad, foul and wicked) of every kind. (James 3:16 NLT)

God wants order in our homes; therefore, both husband and wife must be intentional in keeping these two home-wreckers out. Jealousy makes living together lousy; selfish ambition makes everything about self, and not about us and our families.

People often say, "I am working to provide a home and

stuff for the family." These two issues bring lots of pain, turmoil, disorder, and evil into a home. Believe me, we have been to this place as a family, and it is not good at all. We are thankful for God's mercy and grace to allow us to see and walk away from this destructive place. God's plan is to cherish and keep you as long as you live:

> But the wisdom from above is first pure.
> It is also peace loving, gentle at all times,
> and willing to yield to others. It is full of
> mercy and the fruit of good deeds. It shows
> no favoritism and is always sincere. (James
> 3:17 NLT)

Maintaining this place means cultivating an environment that welcomes the presence of God through prayer and worship. It is a daily invitation to God that asks Him to live and abide in your home. Fervent prayer of a righteous man or woman avails much.

Living to learn is part of the journey to align with the Lord's desires. I am glad I was given a divine motivation to learn, and that has helped build endurance in me. When I accepted Jesus Christ as my Lord and Savior, my appetite for learning grew exponentially. In my bedroom, I would open my pocket-sized Gideon Bible and read Psalms and Proverbs. That was the beginning of diving into the scriptures.

I would circle up with my friends in my living room. They had all accepted Christ. The preacher who was leading the study asked each of us to read a scripture. As each person read, I was amazed at the reading skills of some of them. When it was my turn to read, I could not read well. I was deeply embarrassed. That day, I decided to learn to read much more fluently. My determination to learn to read and write has helped me align with God's plan to become an author. It still blows my mind that the Lord gave me the ability to write my fourth book. When we align with the talents and abilities given to us by God, and we use our gifts to advance His kingdom, we align with our life's purpose. We then get to witness God's glory and see the harvest of souls and the making of disciples. When we live our lives for Jesus, we leave legacies of leadership.

Jesus is serious about the use of our gifts and abilities (Matthew 25:14–30 NLT). It is called stewardship of what has been bestowed upon each person. Jesus holds us accountable to grow and multiply ourselves with the abilities he has endowed us with. When a person does not use the gifts that were given to them, Jesus calls them wicked and lazy servants because they did not put the time, energy, and effort into building up interest. Jesus said this useless person will be put into darkness where there is weeping and gnashing of teeth. However, the person who uses their gifts and talents faithfully will be entrusted with more gifts that will empower, encourage, and equip others to be faithful with their God-given abilities. A man or woman who maximizes their God-given gifts will discover fulfillment and blessings.

God places a high value on utilizing our gifts and abilities. God gives everyone abilities, but the key is the availability of your abilities. We have a responsibility to use our God-given abilities and double our efforts to become the people God has created us to be. God has given us the gift of leadership. I am learning and growing in my leadership effectiveness every day by studying coaches, pastors, leaders of the Bible, and effective leaders in education, military, and business. I also position myself around kingdom leaders who have a track record of integrity in their leadership.

When the Lord told Vickie and me to move to Colorado in 1995, we had no idea that this obedience would align us with our life's purpose—and multiply our efforts in helping people discover their divine purposes in life. We had no idea I would work for Dr. James Dobson, the president of Focus on the Family, which helped align us with excellent children's books, videos, and audio tools that enhance child development, family love, and strong marriages.

I also learned from a best-selling author, Dutch Sheets, who sold more than a million copies of his book on intercessory prayer. He included a story in his book about my hike with young leaders to the summit of Pikes Peak—a thirteen-mile ascent to the top of a 14,110-foot mountain.

I was able to work as the state coordinator for Colorado for the National Day of Prayer, which led to meeting Shirley Dobson, the president of the National Day of Prayer. I never knew I would work for nearly three years at the Billy Graham Evangelistic Association. I served as the state coordinator for Colorado and traveled around America to lay the groundwork for Franklin Graham to preach at crusades throughout the United States.

Next came my exciting window of time serving with the Denver Broncos on their security team, and then I was asked to serve with them at Super Bowl XXXVII, which was a dream come true. Vickie and I were very thankful for the help of Focus on the Family in assisting us in the launch of our first curriculum for our ministry. This was followed by Dutch Sheets and Mike and Cindy Jacobs listening to the vision God downloaded to us, praying for us, and investing in helping us launch the Destiny Project ministry in 1997.

To align your leadership, you must take the first step in adjusting your attitude, which is how we think, and then we are to act by stepping out in faith—to amplify God's agenda so that we advance and achieve His divine purpose.

In closing this chapter, we must take a solid look at why marriage and family are under fire:

> In the same way, you wives must accept the authority of your husbands. Then, even if some refuse to obey the good news, your godly lives will speak to them without any words. They will be won over by observing your pure and reverent lives. Don't be concerned about the outward beauty of fancy hairstyles, expensive jewelry, or beautiful clothes. You should clothe yourselves instead with the beauty that comes from within, the unfading beauty of a gentle and quiet spirit, which is so precious to God. This is how the holy women of old made themselves beautiful. They trusted God and accepted the authority of their husbands. For instance, Sarah obeyed her husband, Abraham, and called him master. You are her daughters when you do what is right without fear of what your husbands might do. In the same way, you husbands must give honor to your wives. Treat them with understanding as you live together. She may be weaker than you are, but she is your equal partner in God's gift of new life. Treat her as you should so your prayers will not be hindered. Finally, all of you should be of one mind. Sympathize with each other. Love each other as brothers and sisters. Be tenderhearted and keep a humble attitude. Don't repay evil for evil. Don't retaliate with insults when people insult you.

Instead, pay back with a blessing. That is what God has called you to do, and he will bless you for it. For the scriptures say "If you want to enjoy life and see many happy days keep your tongue from evil and your lips from telling lies. Turn away from evil and do good. Search for peace, and work to maintain it. The eyes of the Lord watch over those who do right, and his ears are open to their prayers. But the Lord turns his face against those who do evil." (1 Peter 3:1–12 NLT)

There are several points to unpack in this text, and the first is the principle of submission, which simply shows the husband and wife coming into agreement on God's direction and governance of how the home will be governed. When husband and wife are in reverence to God's Word, will, and ways, the home abides under divine blessing and protection. Both husband and wife have key roles in keeping harmony in the home. Wives must conduct themselves with a gentle and respectful attitude, which God says is very precious in His sight, and the husbands must be understanding of their wives, give them honor, and recognize that their emotions are fragile and that they are partners in this grace walk in Christ.

God desires that the husband and the wife should be of one mind, compassionate, tenderhearted, loving, not doing evil for evil, courteous, and understanding. When we follow God's pattern, we inherit blessings. And lastly, if we want to enjoy life and see good days, we must refrain our tongues from speaking evil and seek and pursue peace. God's eyes are always on His people, and His ears are always open to our prayers.

This book is loaded with amazing truth. Our society has been dictating that men should be soft and passive and that women should be hard and aggressive, which is the opposite of what God designed. God made men from the earth, and women are custom-made from the tender side of Adam. Men are designed to construct and be in the dirt, working hard in the elements. God made women to be nurturing and treated with love and tender kindness. God holds a man accountable for how he treats his wife and family, and God holds the wife accountable for her response and respect to her husband.

God hold husbands and fathers to a high standard and said to the man, "Treat her as you should so your prayers will not be hindered" (1 Peter 3:7 NLT).

God held men to a higher standard of behavior when He said, "Don't deal treacherously with the wife of your youth" (Malachi 2:14–15 NKJV).

God expects men not to be bitter toward their wives.

Lastly, God made man first and from the dirt, and the woman was made second and from the side of man. The man of the home has lots of responsibility to cover his family:

> His preaching will turn the hearts of fathers to their children, and the hearts of children to their fathers. Otherwise, I will come and strike the earth with a curse. (Malachi 4:6 NLT)

Overall, God has placed order in the home that brings blessing or curses upon the family. It is not about rank; it is about God's order of headship. Here are the three S's of leadership that must be in the home.

Service

The husband and wife must serve one another and others to advance the purpose God has for them.

Submission

The husband and wife must come into agreement on the order and plan that God has for the family. When God reveals his direction to the husband, there should be cooperation, and when God speaks to the wife, there should be cooperation.

Sex

Sex is vital in the marriage. It brings pleasure and a bonding that release stress and unifies the couple. This intimate act is vitally important to God and vitally important to warding off temptation. Both husband and wife must choose life and decide to follow God's Word, will, and way.

> Today I have given you the choice between life and death, between blessings and curses. Now I call on heaven and earth to witness the choice you make. Oh, that you would choose life, so that you and your descendants might live! You can make this choice by loving the Lord your God, obeying him, and committing yourself firmly to him. This is the key to your life. And if you love and obey the Lord, you will live long in the land the Lord swore to give your ancestors Abraham, Isaac, and Jacob. (Deuteronomy 30:19–20 NLT).

These verses make our choices and decisions up close and personal. God said heaven and earth will watch our choices. God clearly tells us the choice in all seasons and stages is to be life and not death, blessings and not curses. Theses life choices will bless our descendants with life and blessings.

When we practice being calm amid chaos, we have a higher chance of being aligned with the Holy Spirit. When we are coolheaded and avoid fits of rage, we increase our opportunities to hear the voice of the Lord. When we are calm and collected, we multiply our chances of being in a win-win scenario—holding ourselves together and avoiding destructive and volatile situations. When we are caring for our families and others, we improve the bonding of friendships that last a lifetime. The war between the flesh and the spirit is the constant battle we face; therefore, it is imperative to live a life of prayer and studying the scriptures. We must be aligned in the flesh and in the spirit:

> But if you are always biting and devouring one another, watch out! Beware of destroying one another. So, I say, let the Holy Spirit guide your lives. Then you won't be doing what your sinful nature craves. The sinful nature wants to do evil, which is just the opposite of what the Spirit wants. And the Spirit gives us desires that are the opposite of what the sinful nature desires. These two forces are constantly fighting each other, so you are not free to carry out your good intentions. But when you are directed by the Spirit, you are not under obligation to the law of Moses. When you follow your sinful desires of your sinful nature, the results

are very clear: sexual immorality, impurity, lustful pleasures, idolatry, sorcery, hostility, quarreling, jealousy, outbursts of anger, selfish ambition, dissension, division, envy, drunkenness, wild parties, and other sins like these. Let me tell you again, as I have before, that anyone living that sort of life will not inherit the kingdom of God. But the Holy Spirit produces this kind of fruit in our lives: love, joy, peace, patience, kindness, goodness, faithfulness, gentleness, and self-control. There is no law against these things! Those who belong to Christ Jesus have nailed the passions and desires of their sinful nature to His cross and crucified them there. Since we are living by the Spirit, let us follow the Spirit's leading in every part of our lives. Let us not become conceited, or provoke one another, or be jealous of one another. (Galatians 5:15–26 NLT)

When we are with the spirit, the kingdom advances—and we experience heavenly moments and victory. When we are with the flesh, we experience outright fleshly moments.

- Inappropriate sexual behavior includes immorality such as adultery, fornication, homosexuality, lesbianism, intercourse with animals, intercourse with close relations, sexual intercourse with a divorced man or woman, impurity, uncleanness and lustful licentiousness, porn and indecent and promiscuous behavior, and unprincipled sexual matters or behavior.

- Inappropriate anger includes strife, jealously, anger, outbursts of rage or selfishness, dissension, factions, envy.
- Inappropriate substance abuse includes drunkenness, sorcery, and carousing.
- Demonic strongholds include idolatry, sorcery, and envy.

Our culture has become inundated with pleasure—without having a conscience. The godly family must demonstrate what is God's original design so that families can see and witness what God has planned for the marriage and family. We must point to God's heavenly direction, which includes love, joy, peace, long-suffering, gentleness, goodness, meekness, faith, and self-control.

The goal of this chapter is help us understand and define boundaries of love and respect for one another. Families must establish healthy directions and frameworks and set up custom plans for their families. We all must be on the right course with God and learn His pace and walk in stride with His plan for our families. Let us build upon these family foundations of love.

This is God's ultimate agenda:

> For God loved the world (Greek word *kosmos* meaning inhabitants, men, the human family, orderly arrangement that influence society, the whole circle of earthly goods, endowments riches, advantages, pleasures.) so much that he gave (Greek word *didomi* meaning bestowed a gift of adventure) His one

> and only Son, so that everyone who believes
> (Greek word *pisteuo* meaning to commit one's
> trust.) in Him will not perish (Greek word
> *appollymi* meaning destroy, die, or lose,) but
> have eternal life. (John 3:16 NLT)

Let us receive God's Son and implement the joy of the Lord into our homes, which will give us strength to continue moving into God's plan and direction. Let us appropriate God's peace, which is healthy for everyone's well-being and comfort. Let us understand long-suffering, which is the grounding force of life, involving pain, disappointment, health challenges, and brokenness in our lives. Let's keep ourselves in the vitality of God's grace, where we rely on God's divine assistance to come through life's challenges.

Gentleness is speaking softly words, which is a big winner over being harsh, loud, or yelling. Goodness will have a huge victory in overcoming evil, and meekness is exercising good judgment and control mixed with humility. When you have the right authority to react to a situation, you have the authority to command.

Faith is staying aligned with God's Word and having the confidence that God backs His Word and promises and knowing He is contending and fighting for what is rightfully yours. Lastly, with temperance, which is self-control, you will recognize that you can grab hold of yourself—and no force can make you do what is wrong. It is also recognizing that you must be disciplined, control your impulses, reactions, and responses, and keep your pants up in moments of great temptation.

Seven Points of Alignment

1. Action is leadership with results.
2. Attitude determines altitude.
3. Achievement is believing in yourself.
4. Agenda is aligning with God's plan and purpose.
5. Amplify your personality and gifts to glorify God.
6. Adjustment is being flexible to move in a different direction.
7. Advancing is moving forward with God's plan and strategy.

Elevate Questions

1. Why is this principle of alignment important regarding God's kingdom?
2. Why was Peter awestruck by the large catch of fish?
3. What motivating factor caused Coach Rex to learn to read and write?
4. Why is using your gifts an especially important principle in God's kingdom?
5. How does a train parallel with alignment?
6. What is submission all about?
7. What are the three S's of a strong marriage?

Proclaiming Alignment

1. I am pursuing and walking in God's perfect will.
2. I recognize and follow the voice of the Good Shepherd.
3. I decree that we are aligned with God's plan in every season of our lives in Jesus's name.
4. I declare that we know God's will and that we are stepping into all God has intended in Jesus's name.
5. I declare that we are on God's frequency and timing to advance forward with His perfect will in Jesus's name.

6. I declare that my family will be on the same frequency and will obey God's Word, will, and ways during times of transition in Jesus's name.
7. We will speak life to one another and enjoy the fruit of our words in Jesus's name.

Prayers of Alignment

1. Lord, help us to be fruitful and produce results in Jesus's name (John 15:4 NLT).
2. Lord, help us to be aligned in Your Word so that we are positioned with our gifts and abilities to receive miracles, blessings, and breakthroughs in Jesus's name (Luke 5:1–11 NLT).
3. Help us daily to be in step with you so that we can be unified and in agreement with your daily agenda in Jesus's name (Amos 3:3 NLT).
4. Lord, help us keep an obedient attitude so that we are always in position to receive Your bountiful blessings in Jesus's name (Isaiah 1:19 NLT).
5. Lord, help us to be ready and positioned to win daily battles in Jesus's name (Nehemiah 4:13–14 NLT).
6. Lord, help us deal with all fears that the enemy attempts to put on us and help us stay in the force of faith, and obliterate demonic assignments (Job 3:25 NLT).
7. Father, may we choose life and blessing everyday of our lives in Jesus's name (Deuteronomy 30:19–20 NLT).

TRANSITION

STAYING IN STEP WITH GOD'S PLAN AND PURPOSE

Transition is defined as the process of changing from one state to another. To move, transform, shift, jump, or leap—change is necessary for growth. Transition and change must happen to get us to the next place God has planned for us.

Transition is defined as the process, passage, or period of changing from one state, stage, or condition to another. Phillip was transitioned to another place after sharing the Gospel. Transition is not always easy, but it is necessary to elevate to the next level in Christ. Throughout our lives, we are transitioning from birth, infancy, toddler, adolescence, teen years, adulthood, single, married, to having children, to having grandchildren, and to growing old. In this age we are living in, many sectors of society are hostile to biblical truth. Christ followers must remain coolheaded, calm, collected, and composed. To be successful with the basics, the four C's are required to remain self-controlled when people are hostile because of our beliefs and biblical standards of living.

Transition requires a steady focus so that you do not become distracted from the task God has called and assigned you to do. It can be catastrophic when parents fail to navigate their families through the treacherous times of our modern-day culture. Husbands and wives must pay attention to the warning signs and take a time-out to stop, pray, and rest. Every family must seek God to understand the direction He is leading their family. Every family has a unique design, direction, and destiny that must be understood. When families are devoted to God and His Word, there will greater discernment of what God is calling a family to do.

We must be prepared for the unexpected and learn to adapt to unwanted changes that are a part of life. Substance abuse, financial challenges, fatigue, family fights, arguments, and a lack of knowledge and understanding have destroyed many families. When families are sidetracked with life issues, they can become less attentive to God's Word and plan:

> You also must be ready all the time, for the
> Son of Man will come when least expected.
> (Matthew 24:44 NLT)

We must daily be ready to transition from this earth since none of us are promised tomorrow.

> How do you know what your life will be like
> tomorrow? Your life is like the morning fog
> it's here a little while then it's gone. (James
> 4:14 NLT)

Therefore, we must live by God's Word, love our families and friends, and share the Gospel in every opportunity we have so that the people we encounter can also be ready for eternity.

As in the case with Nehemiah, God put a burden on his heart for Jerusalem whose land was destroyed and desolate. In Nehemiah 6:3–4 (NLT), we see seven areas where Satan attempts to distract Nehemiah from doing God's will. If he cannot distract us, he tries to delay us. If he can't delay us, he tries to discredit us. If that does not work, he tries division. If that does not work, he tries domination. If that does not work, he uses his most common weapon: deception. No matter what is thrown at us, we must keep building and advancing God's work.

> I replied by sending this message to them: "I am engaged in a great work, so I can't come. Why should I stop working to come and meet with you?" Four times they sent the same message and each time I gave the same reply. (Nehemiah 6:3–4 NLT)

As we see in this text, the enemy used many tactics to attempt to get Nehemiah off track. Transition is simply staying focused on the course before you and getting to the goal as quickly as possible. When a leader is focused, momentum is created in the leader and the team to help shift everyone to victory. Nehemiah took responsibility to stay focused and stay the course with the project. When you are immersed in a project, you literally need to do everything you can to stay focused and utilize all the resources available to you.

In my senior year of high school, I was experiencing an amazing time with my academics, attitude adjustments, and athletics. I knew I had to do well in geometry and French, keep out of trouble, be respectful of my leaders, and excel in sports. At the beginning of my track season, while running the two hundred meters, I was running around three-quarter speed; suddenly, I had a burst of energy as though I had been jolted with power. Like a turbocharge, I shifted to a much faster speed, which I had never experienced before. I won the race that day and set a school record. In an instant, I went from mediocre runner to a premier sprinter. That is what I call transition. Like Nehemiah, there many variables that were trying to pull me from my divine course. I knew I wanted to attend college on a scholarship.

When the moment came for me to sign my letter of intent to attend Western Carolina University, my life transitioned again. I would be leaving home, going to a new place, and starting on a new journey. I wish I had been more prepared for what would be on the other side of this transition. Some things were exciting, and some were not so exciting.

During my first day on campus, they began timing all the new football recruits in the forty-yard dash. Prior to my run, the coaches had announced the times of the other runners. I would hear speeds of 4.8, 4.7, 4.6, and 4.5 seconds. When the time came for me to run the forty-yard dash, I had no idea that my whole life was going to change. I would soon be known as the fastest person on the entire team. That day, I ran the forty-yard dash in 4.3 and later 4.2 seconds. Every coach and player knew who I was that day because I had run faster than everyone and had the fastest time. What came with that recognition was respect and ridicule. My confidence was so high that I felt I could play in the NFL, and I made the mistake of saying that to someone who I thought was my friend. When I said that, it was not meant to be shared with others. Unfortunately, that comment got back to the upperclassmen.

Just like Joseph, we must be careful about what we say and to whom we say it. When you do something extraordinary, people who are secure in themselves rejoice with you and want to help you and themselves become better. However, those who are insecure can become bitter and jealous; they may develop an unhealthy competitiveness instead of trying to improve their lives. They want to disprove your life, and they want you to fail—whether it be in sports, education, government, media, military, business, church, or family. There is no place for jealously, envy, or bitterness. A successful transition requires a positive attitude and focus. When you are moving with God's plan and purpose, you don't need extra weight that slows you down.

> Therefore, since we are surrounded by such a huge crowd of witnesses to the life of faith, let us strip off every weight that slows us down, especially the sin that so easily trips us up. And let us run with endurance the race God has set before us. (Hebrews 12:1 NLT)

> So do not throw away this confident trust in the Lord. Remember the great reward it brings you! Patient endurance is what you need now, so that you will continue to do God's will. Then you will receive all that he has promised. (Hebrews 10:35–36 NLT)

These verses have been a constant reminder to me. They remind me not to give up or lose confidence in God's ability to work in my life and my family. When we are aligned with God's plan, we can move more rapidly and more efficiently, just as a car that has been aligned moves much more efficiently and smoothly. When a car is aligned, it gets better mileage— and there is less wear and tear on the vehicle. When families are lined up according to God's design, everyone is aware of their roles, responsibilities, and purposes. So, how do we remain aligned in God? Each of us must take responsibility for learning how God wants us aligned with Him, which requires staying in daily communion with our first love: God. It also helps when we are consistent in our daily devotions and church attendance.

> So faith comes from hearing, that is, hearing the good news about Christ. (Romans 10:17 NLT)

Marriages must be aligned in covenant with God, and to be in covenant, we must grasp what a covenant is all about. Marriage is a binding agreement between two parties under oath to perform certain duties toward each other. God's desire is for marriage to represent Him. God desires marriage for reproduction, and God desires for marriage to take dominion. When we are following these designs, we are properly aligned with God's Word, will, and way.

All married couples should have a statement of commitment written down and review their statement of faith on a regular basis to remain focused and purposeful. Families must clearly respect and be sensitive to family traditions and growing together with love and grace because children leave and develop their own families. Married couples must decide how children will be disciplined. There are many details and transitions in life, including date nights, chores, balancing checkbooks, cooking, helping with homework, school visits, spending accountability, planning vacations, medical and dental checkups, auto maintenance, and grocery shopping. There is also spiritual leadership, such as family Bible time, prayer and fasting, church attendance, and giving tithes and offerings.

When a man prays for and with his wife, her greatest needs are meet by God—and unity and harmony are stronger.

Transition under Fire!

Vickie went from running as secretary of our county's Republican Party to being the chair of the county's Republican Party—and our county is one the largest Republican districts in the nation. Through all the ups and downs that come with politics, Vickie had no idea she would be elected to secretary and then voted in as the chair of the El Paso County Republican Party nine months later. Talk about transition! We had no idea that this transition was going to take us to new levels of trials and tests—as well as ridicule and ruthlessness from some people and some leaders in our city, county, and state. Being involved in politics is quite hard and can be painful and disenchanting. It includes the bombardment of criticism, tireless hours of work, and brutal attacks packed with lies and deception. You might think you have the right people on the bus, but you quickly learn they are working against you to discredit and destroy you. Who can you really trust in this arena? So many agendas, so many lies—and leadership positions hang in the balance.

John Maxwell said, "Everything rises and falls on leadership." In this situation, it seems to be blatantly evident. When a good leader quits, there is a void for bad leadership to quickly fill; this allows them to multiply their wicked and evil agendas. Therefore, good and called leaders must hold the line under insurmountable pressure and ridicule. They must be ready to step into positions of leadership, which requires a new breed of leaders who are bold and courageous for God.

In Acts 8:29–39 (NLT), God quickly transitioned Phillip to another city when he completed the divine assignment. I call this a *supernatural transition*. When Phillip heard God's instructions, He showed the eunuch the meaning of the scriptures, which brought insight and encouragement, and love was demonstrated when Phillip stopped and took the time to explain and pray with the eunuch to receive Jesus. This should be our goal as we transition from home to work or to the market or to any other place we are going. We must be ready to help point people to Christ. We need to be ready in every seaon. Wherever God has positioned us, our number one goal is to bring God's kingdom into that arena and be ready to share and explain the Gospel to everyone who desires to know Jesus.

Every family must decide who they will serve. The Tonkins family has decided—just as Joshua decided—that we will live and serve God.

The call now is for sold-out Christ followers to transition our thinking to get involved in the government arena. Legislators can impact the culture of a community, city, county, and state. Legislation can help improve family life or hurt it, and those involved in government can approve or disapprove of it. If we want to help protect future generations, we must be involved in helping direct legislation that protects family values.

Our fundamental values are being threatened by those who desire to harm our families and our futures, and our children are being threatened with ideas that can turn their hearts and minds against the values we hold dear. If their plans and ideas are implemented, it will have harmful ramifications that can destroy our young people's identities and purposes in life. We must be involved in the systems that directly impact our families and children. Yes, the political realm is a cesspool of lies, deceit, and deception; therefore, leaders who know God must stand in the gap and bring God's kingdom's agenda into this arena. Though ridiculously difficult, it's timely and extremely necessary. We must not avoid engaging the government system. We must first go into any arena with much prayer, wisdom, and knowledge from the Lord.

During times of transition, we must safely pass the baton to the next generation with the knowledge of God's righteous ways. If we don't make the transfer, we could lose valuable keys in the transition to the next generation. We must study all of God's keys to the kingdom so that we disciple a generation with these kingdom keys of success and victory.

Prayer is the rocket fuel that pushes and thrusts us to the next level of God's purpose and destiny.

> You guide me with Your counsel, leading me to a glorious destiny. Whom have I in heaven but You? I desire You more than anything on earth. My health may fail, and my spirit may grow weak, but God remains the strength of my heart; He is mine forever. (Psalm 73:24–26 NLT)

We all will transition into eternity, and what you decide to do here on earth regarding your soul will determine where you spend your eternal destiny. When we give our whole hearts to Jesus and surrender our wills to His will, we will spend our eternal destiny in heaven with God. Decide today to make Jesus the Lord of your life by confessing with your mouth the Lord Jesus and believing in your heart that you raised Jesus from the dead. When you have made this confession with all sincerity and believe with all your heart, you shall be saved—and your name will be written in the Lamb's book of life.

I want to share this story of the ultimate transition from earth to eternity. I had no idea that my oldest brother, Alvin, was going to transition to heaven on May 23, 2020. I cannot put into proper words the shock, grief, and pain I felt and continue to feel in the loss of my brother. We did not have an opportunity to say goodbye because there were no signs or warnings.

My sister Terecia called on a Saturday afternoon and said, "Alvin is gone."

I was in disbelief and couldn't wrap my mind around it. I cried for days, weeks, and months. I highly encourage you to cherish the time with your loved ones and to spend time with them as much as possible because one day, each of us will leave this earth and enter eternity.

As I write this, the moment is still fresh in my mind. We had his funeral and homegoing service on May 29, 2020. I shared how he led me to Christ and how he was so respected in his community and with his coworkers. He was an excellent husband of thirty-eight years, a father of eight, and a well-respected electrician. I deeply miss him and dedicate this book to my brother Alvin. He was an excellent example of a godly man, husband, and father.

Seven Points of Transition
1. Timing and transition are vital to the success of a journey.
2. Toughness to the enemy is necessary, and tenderness to family is necessary in transition.
3. Trusting God is imperative during transition.
4. Tact is vitally necessary in knowing when to say the right thing at the right time.
5. Transforming your thinking helps you adjust in times of transition.
6. Talents must be maximized during transition.
7. Training and being physically fit minimize injuries during transitions.

Prayer empowers us to transition to the next level with great confidence. We must transition into a place of peace in God—discovering purpose and receiving prophetic vision—so that we are positioned to win victories. When we are victorious, we elevate to new places of leadership.

> Stay alert! Watch out for your great enemy, the devil. He prowls around like a roaring lion, looking for someone to devour. (1 Peter 5:8 NLT)

Elevate Questions

1. Why is transition necessary?
2. Do you listen well enough to help resolve issues in your family (James 1:19 NLT)?
3. What is the difference between order and chaos in the home?
4. What does divine order look like in the home?
5. Have you experienced chaos in your home?
6. What examples did you find helpful of Coach Rex's high school and college stories?
7. Why is timing vitally necessary during transition?

God's divine order means everyone recognizes God as Lord of the household. There is mutual respect, authority is recognized and exercised, and everyone knows what is required of them. God's Word and prayer are at the center of the home. There is love and courtesy.

With a home in chaos, disrespect is high. No one follow God's Word or His divine authority. The father is not leading spiritually, the mother despises authority and usurps the authority, and the children have no boundaries and run the home. No one cleans, no one respects, and the home is centered on the television. There is rudeness and no thoughtfulness.

Prayers during Transition

1. Father, help us to be ready to transition when it is our time in Jesus's name (Matthew 24:44 NLT).

2. Father, help us stay focused on the purpose and task at hand and help us recognize and discern the distractions and deceptions of our enemies in Jesus's name (Nehemiah 6:1–15 NLT).

3. Lord, help us get rid of the sins that slow us down and help us run light so that we stay in step with Your timing in Jesus's name (Hebrews 12:19 NLT).

4. Lord, give us the endurance and confidence we need to be positioned to receive your promises in Jesus's name (Hebrews 10:35–36 NLT).

5. Lord, help us to be instant in season and out of season to share the love of Christ with people who are lost and hurting in Jesus's name (Acts 8:29–39 NLT).

6. Lord, guide us to the glorious destiny you have planned for us. When we fall short, help us to lean on your strength in Jesus's name (Psalm 73:24–26 NLT).

7. Lord, may we learn to be alert and watchful of our enemy who seeks for ways to destroy us. Thank You for this holy alertness in Jesus's name (1 Peter 5:8 NLT).

EXCEL

YOU HAVE A DESTINY!

Excel is defined as the quality of being outstanding or extremely good and exhibiting brilliance, greatness, caliber, skill, and mastery. We must master the skills and gifts given to us by God. God does not want us to be mediocre and dull. He wants us to be excelling and creative through the inspiration of the Holy Spirit. Proper prayer produces power and positive results. In studying this verse, I have noticed the key components of excelling.

> Do you see a man who excels in his work?
> He will stand before kings; he will not stand
> before unknown men. (Proverbs 22:29
> NKJV)

This verse in the Hebrew translation speaks loudly to me. The word "see" in Hebrew is *chazah*, which means perceive, look, or to have vision, real sight of divine presence. The word "excel" in Hebrew is *mahiyr*, which means skilled, quick, prompt, apt, and ready. The word "work" in Hebrew is *melakak*, which means service, public business, political, religious, occupation, public affairs, property, or wealth.

You have permission to be yourself and excel. You do not have to apologize for the work you put in to be great. Jesus told you to let your light shine so that people can see your good deeds.

> You are the light of the world like a city on a hilltop that cannot be hidden. No one lights a lamp and then puts it under a basket. Instead, a lamp is placed on a stand, where it gives light to everyone in the house. In the same way, let your good deeds shine out for all to see, so that everyone will praise your heavenly Father. (Matthew 5:14–16 NLT)

I like this verse because it reminds me of my life's calling to help people discover their purpose, their reason for living, and their destinies, which means fulfilling your intended journey in life.

How did Daniel excel? What habits did Daniel develop to help him excel privately and publicly? Why did the Bible say he had an excellent spirit? I believe Daniel had an awareness that all wisdom and intelligence comes from God.

Daniel's position and posture about prayer placed him in a position to receive God's prophetic insight and wisdom. When we understand that time alone with God helps build our relationship with God—and as we are faithful—the Lord anoints us to excel in divine and holy assignments. Also, Daniel did his part by devoting himself to the reading and studying of God's Word, which publicly showed he approved of God.

> "This man Daniel, whom the king named Belteshazzar has exceptional ability and is filled with divine knowledge and

understanding. He can interpret dreams, explain riddles, and solve difficult problems. Call for Daniel, and he will tell you what the writing means." So Daniel was brought in before the king. The king asked him, "Are you Daniel, one of the exiles brought from Judah by my predecessor, King Nebuchadnezzar? I have heard that you have the spirit of the gods within you and that you are filled with insight, understanding, and wisdom." (Daniel 5:12–14 NLT)

Daniel soon proved himself more capable than all the other administrators and high officers. Because of Daniel's great ability, the king made plans to place him over the entire empire. (Daniel 6:3 NLT)

Daniel was given five exceptional attributes: exceptional ability; divine knowledge and understanding; the ability to interpret dreams; the ability to explain riddles, and the ability to solve difficult problems. Excellence begins with a discovery of the exceptional ability and the skills bestowed upon us from God.

What is your exceptional ability?

Daniel was filled with divine knowledge and understanding; his prayer life and studying of the scriptures gave evidence of this. We must utilize our time wisely and make the most of our time to study and spend time in prayer daily.

Interpreting dreams was another gift. If we have not developed this attribute, we must ask God for discernment to help us explain things that are hard to comprehend. Daniel explained riddles, explained difficult puzzles, and solved problems. What problems has God assigned for you to solve with your abilities, understanding, and skills?

Leaders who excel are good at solving difficult problems. When we are faithful with the things of God—like His Word, prayer, and obedience—He can elevate us into influential positions that help expand His kingdom and bring glory to His name. When we share God's wisdom and insights, we position ourselves to excel, elevate ourselves to new opportunities to lead, and bring in God's righteousness. We must impart rich principles to people who are desiring to learn and grow.

> You have heard me teach things that have been confirmed by many reliable witnesses. Now teach these truths to other trustworthy people who will be able to pass on to others. (2 Timothy 2:2 NLT)

When we learn biblical truths and the principles of success, we must share them with others. I believe Daniel excelled because he was dedicated to following the Lord and because he incorporated the Lord in every part of his life.

> And so, dear brothers and sisters, I plead with you to give your bodies to God because of all He has done for you. Let them be a living and holy sacrifice—the kind He will find acceptable. This is truly the way to worship Him. Don't copy the behavior and customs of this world, but let God transform you into a new person by changing the way you think. Then you will learn to know God's will for

you, which is good and pleasing and perfect.
(Romans 12:1–2 NLT)

One hundred percent devotion and dedication to God positions us to fulfill our destinies with excellent spirits.

Our standard of excellence should be higher for ourselves than what we require from others. To excel to your destiny requires a fire in your belly, and in your mind, you must have a strong desire to succeed. My motto in college was "You gotta want it." To truly excel, you must have the want to inside of you. You have to be hungry and thirsty to spend time with the Most High God. He is excellent in all His ways. You need the desire to grow and enter God's fullness. You must have the drive to fulfill what you were born to do and do it with your best efforts in mind.

To excel, leaders must know what is required of them and what will help attain the best return and the best results. To excel is learning to pace oneself to elevate to new levels of influence. Excelling is knowing your purpose, fulfilling that purpose with passion, utilizing God's principles and leading people with God's vision. Excelling requires a heart of service and not control, utilizing your place of authority to help empower people. Joshua's attitude of service and submission to Moses caused him to emerge into a powerful position of leadership. Joshua was dedicated to the study and mediation of scripture day and night.

> Study this book of instruction continually. Meditate on it day and night so you will be sure to obey everything written in it. Only then will you prosper and succeed in all you do. (Joshua 1:8 NLT)

To excel requires us to know what is needed. What assets or resources are available? What are the abilities of the people involved? What are the attitudes of the people who are willing? And what has been accomplished by those who can get things done? A great coach will discover the best players and put them in the positions to excel, which helps the entire team excel. No matter a player's color, creed or culture, a great coach will put into the game the players who demonstrate character, commitment, communication, outright hard work, and the heart to give their absolute best. A great coach also knows how to utilize every team member in their strength zone to help the team win and succeed.

My coach would evaluate his team's assets each year, and he knew what was needed. My respect for my coach during a moment of testing and embarrassment at a track meet helped me make the decision to submit to his authority. However, later in my high school career, my decision to yield and obey my leaders led me to emerge as the captain of the track team. Also, my submission to run the four hundred meters, which I had no desire to run, later paid dividends for me, allowing me to become the conference, sectional, regional champion, and the state runner-up clocking in at 48.2 in the four hundred meters. This led me to college track and running the forty-yard dash in 4.2 seconds, which was amazing acceleration for a boy from Greensboro, North Carolina.

What is very cool about the Destiny Project organization is that we give young people and leaders an opportunity to perform through service, sports, and leadership training. If you are committed and dedicated, we see that, and when you are not committed, we see that too. The Destiny Project provides practical insights that will enhance your spiritual development. The Destiny Project allows us to coach people along in their journey of life. We have coaches who are excellent at instructing, equipping, encouraging, and empowering. We also reward character, hard work, teamwork, and hustle at our camps and meetings. We have students strive daily to improve their behavior, performance, and leadership.

To excel, one must take the time to pause or huddle, focus, listen, adjust strategy, and make substitutions. When Daniel was faced with a dilemma, he asked for time and called his prayer partners to pray for wisdom in the matter. God gave them the answer to solve the king's problems. If we genuinely want to excel, we must give people permission to help us, correct us, show the correct way of doing a task or adjusting an attitude, and ask for feedback. To excel, you must learn to have fun while doing what are tasked to do. When you enjoy what you do, it does not feel like work. We must learn to be creative in the endeavors assigned to us; we must learn God's perspective and gain wisdom in doing our best.

To truly excel is to dedicate one's life to Jesus, enduring hardships, serving our families and communities, making the most of our time, and navigating though life's problems and challenges. How we utilize our skills is important to God.

How did Joseph excel?

> The Lord was with Joseph, so he succeeded in
> everything he did as he served in the home of
> Egyptian master. (Genesis 39:2 NLT)

He had a divine assignment upon his life, and God downloaded dreams and visions and gave him the gift of leadership. Joseph desired to honor God by living a life of honest work and integrity. Joseph had his father's parental blessings and support.

What made Esther so effective in saving her people? Esther's stunning beauty positioned her to be chosen for royal leadership. She also honored the authority of her uncle's divine wisdom and counsel; her divine assignment was strategic in saving a nation. The parallel with leadership is submission, honor, and listening to divine authority, which prepares you for kingdom authority and leadership.

> If you keep quiet at a time like this, deliverance and relief for the Jews will arise from some other place, but you and your relatives will die. Who knows if perhaps you were made queen for just such a time as this? (Esther 4:14 NLT)

If you are in a position of leadership that influences life and death via legislation that protects the family and biblical values, you have a responsibility to bring God's kingdom to that position.

> This is my command be strong and courageous! Do not be afraid or discouraged. For the Lord, your God is with you wherever you God. (Joshua 1:9 NLT)

Daniel 6:4–28 (NLT) tells an amazing story of courage in the face of intimidation. When you are excelling, the enemy will use people as puppets to attempt to find fault with you. Daniel was faithful, responsible, and trustworthy. These insecure people will attack your faith to discredit you as we can see so clearly in our political arena. Leaders must be covered in prayer so they can discern plots and plans to attempt to destroy freedoms that give us the ability to live for the Lord as the Word of God directs us. When leaders make laws that restrict our freedom to worship, this gives wicked leaders the unjust right to enforce consequences upon us. Once laws are made, leaders must follow the law they willfully and ignorantly legislated.

> So, King Darius signed the law. But when Daniel learned that the law had been signed, he went home and knelt down as usual in his upstairs room, with its windows open toward Jerusalem. He prayed three times a day, just as he had always done, giving thanks to his God. (Daniel 6:9–10 NLT)

We must remember that no law supersedes God's law. However, we must keep our sole trust in God when we must face the consequences of civil law.

> Then the officials went together to Daniel's house and found him praying and asking for God's help. So they went straight to the king and reminded him about his law. "Did you not sign a law that for the next thirty days any person who prays to anyone, divine or human—except to you, Your Majesty—will be thrown into the den of lions?"
>
> "Yes," the king replied, "that decision stands; it is an official law of the Medes and Persians that cannot be revoked." Then they told the king, "That man Daniel, one of the captives from Judah, is ignoring you and your law. He still prays to his God three times a day." Hearing this, the king was deeply troubled, and he tried to think of a way to save Daniel.

> He Spent the rest of the day looking for a
> way to get Daniel out of this predicament.
> (Daniel 6:11–14 NLT)

Because it was the law, the king ordered Daniel arrested and thrown to the lions. King Darius recognize he had been duped and deceived in bringing harm to Daniel. He called on God for help, prayed all night, and fasted. God's divine protection in the form of an angel protected Daniel from the lions. Those who plot and plan against God's people eventually hang themselves. When we are in positions and places of authority, we can follow King Darius's example.

> Then King Darius sent this message to the
> people of every race and nation and language
> throughout the world: "Peace and prosperity
> to you! I decree that everyone throughout
> my kingdom should tremble with fear before
> the God of Daniel. For He is the living God,
> and He will endure forever. His kingdom
> will never be destroyed, and His rule will
> never end. He rescues and saves His people;
> He performs miraculous signs and wonders
> in the heavens and on earth. He has rescued
> Daniel from the power of the lions." (Daniel
> 6:25–27 NLT)

I was serving as a substitute teacher at my alma mater, Grimsley High School, and I quickly moved to helping with security and working closely with the administration in dealing with discipline. I was not aware that a well-known drug dealer came to campus weekly to distribute drugs. This dealer was very arrogant and prideful. He bragged that the administrators and the school resource officer would never catch him. I was told this had been going on for three years.

I served and walked the school campus to check on teachers and make sure our students were good. Many people on the campus did not know that I was praying and declaring God's Word over the high school while I was walking the school grounds and hallways. I was literally taking ground from the enemy. I believe those prayers led to the biggest drug bust of the year on the Grimsley High School campus. I was told by law enforcement and administrators that this drug dealer saw me walking the grounds and ran right into the school resource officer and administrators. The clincher was that it occurred before he had distributed his drugs.

I was called on the radio by the school resource officer and told to go to the principal's office. I wondered why, but when I arrived, there was a young person with all the drugs laid out on the desk that he had planned to distribute. They told me he got caught because he was trying to avoid me. I immediately turned around and left the office because I had known where this young person was headed for a long time. I was saddened by this because I like to help young people avoid this type of criminal activity. I want to help them excel toward their purpose.

For the next several months, many students thought I was an undercover cop. My wife worked in the library, and students would often ask if her husband was an undercover cop. Even students who did not know that Christian was my son tell him that I was an undercover cop. Because the biggest drug dealer was caught, they gave me the crowning credit for catching him—even though I had no idea who he was or what he was doing. God knew and positioned me, simply because of prayer, and my prayers exposed evil and demonic activity. I excelled as an employee at Grimsley High School because of my prayers and discernment. I was summoned to help uncover plots and to stop potential fights that could have led to riots and destruction. To excel is giving your best, listening for God's Word, and cooperating with God in what He wants to do in your life and the lives of His people.

My desire is to give God my absolute best because I know my days are short and we are not promised tomorrow. I want to be tenacious in building God's kingdom by demonstrating an outstanding work ethic, which is an attribute in excelling in life. I hope my life inspires future generations to reach high above the bar we set and reach for the goal of excellence, which leads us and prepares us all for eternity.

To excel, we must embrace all of God's Word, will, and ways. We must execute God's plan, guard our hearts, and stay on course with our divine destiny. We must make a habit of giving our best and preparing for greatness. When we position ourselves to excel, we will see new levels that we have not experienced before. Excelling helps us grab hold of greater things.

Darryl Moore, a friend and coach from Chesapeake, Virginia, said, "The culture in any organization or team is determined by the worst attitude that the leader is willing to tolerate."

Excellent leadership is having the proper attitude and applying His Word to our lives. We can rest assured that God backs His Word, and with confidence, we can fulfill our purpose and destiny.

Elevate Defining Moment

On May 23, 2020, my sister told me that our oldest brother, Alvin, had died and gone home to Jesus. The shock and disbelief changed everything. We all have been shaken to the core of our beings at one time or another. Amid the shock, pain, grief, and despair, the Lord offered me a mind-boggling assignment.

While I was in North Carolina, Vickie's siblings received a notice that their parents' property needed some work done. If it were not taken care of by May 15, 2020, it would be demolished by county contractors—and the siblings would receive a bill for those services. Since I was already there, I decided to investigate the matter. It was June, and we were obviously past the deadline.

I arranged to meet my cousin, his working partner, and the pastor who lived next door to the property to see if they could help me. In my conversation with them, they did not sound too optimistic. They also cast some doubt about having to work in poison ivy, which was everywhere on the property. Tearing down the building and taking the materials to the landfill would be expensive. I decided to get away to seek God and pray in the mountains near Linville, North Carolina, an area with beautiful waterfalls. After some time and reflection, I realized I had to tackle the assignment with what I had: my time and my physical abilities.

On Sunday, June 7, I arrived at the property and noticed that the neighbor's brother was using his chain saw to cut down the trees that surrounded the property. I purchased a small extended saw that allowed me to cut the low-hanging branches. I spent my first day moving branches to the east side of the property to be staged for burning later in the week.

On day two, the neighbor brought a tractor and moved a whole lot of branches and trees in much less time. It's amazing how much can be accomplished with a tractor. I asked if we could use the tractor to put a chain around the carport's brick columns. They consented, and we successfully pulled down the columns.

On the third day, I began the day by tearing into the carport and cutting the rafters, and then I staged them on the east side of the property. On day four, I felt led to get a sledgehammer. I started at the center of the house on the porch and hit the wall until the bricks began breaking loose. Just like Gideon, I used my strength to the best of my ability—and God sent divine favor and help.

When the neighbors saw me using everything I had, they were moved to help. They brought a tractor to help me take down the rest of the brick walls. I was amazed! On day five, we continued knocking down bricks and cutting down more trees. On day six, I rented a small excavator and started bringing down the structure. On days seven and eight, I continued taking down the structure.

The neighbor, a pastor, began helping me and asked me to be a guest speaker at his church. I ended the day early on Saturday to spend time in prayer and study. Even though I was still mourning the death of my brother and was exhausted from working long hours for seven consecutive days, I said yes.

When I spoke that Sunday morning, the people of God were encouraged by my message. When I ended my speaking, I was asked to go to the lobby to greet the people. As I waited for the senior pastor to dismiss the service, he announced to the congregation that I needed help in tearing down the brick house and clearing the property. If anyone had equipment, he asked them to consider coming to help. This request brought another mind-blowing experience that week. We had two excavators and three trailers hauling the materials to the landfill. We also had a trailer designated for scrap metal that we hauled to the scrapyard.

On the fifteenth day, I called the county inspector. When he arrived, he was amazed that the structure was completely down, and he gave us the okay that the property was in compliance with the county. To God be the glory and for all the help God sent us!

Another amazing moment was that the operators estimated we had delivered sixty tons of materials to the landfill, and the cost per ton was thirty-eight dollars. When they explained our dilemma, they did not charge us one dime. To God be the glory for His magnificent help with this endeavor! We saw God's hand and provision throughout the fifteen days. What started out as an impossible task ended up being a possible task because of a simple act of obedience and using what I had available to mobilize a community to help get the property into compliance. I was so blessed that the body of Christ in that region responded to a need.

Seven Benchmarks for Preparing Yourself to Excel

1. Quality. This means doing your work with neatness, accuracy, and thoroughness. Each day, I did my best to keep the jobsite clean and neat.
2. Productivity. This relates to the volume produced, the response to workload pressure, and the utilization of work time. Each day, there was noticeable progress, and the people in the community were amazed.
3. Dependability. This relates to punctuality, attendance, the degree of direction required, and the planning and organization of the work. Each day, I made the effort to arrive early to prepare for the workday, and I picked up tools, water, ice, and other necessary supplies.
4. Cooperation. This is the ability to work with the public and a team, the attitude toward the job and the ministry, and the willingness to accept guidance. I had to prepare myself to listen to both welcome and unwelcome opinions.

5. Job knowledge. This refers to the bringing about an understanding of job requirements, the ability to think a problem through, and the understanding of related areas. You must learn to be still and wait and take the time to think through the project so that all angles are considered.

6. Communication. This is conveying thoughts clearly through oral and written methods. The ability to communicate clearly with fellow team members is vital. Keeping a positive outlook is a particularly important element because you will often come across negative people—and communicating trust and faith in God sends a clear message that this is a divine assignment.

7. Leadership. This is suggesting new and better methods for the development of the team. Leaders must be aware of the attitude and morale of the group. A great leader must develop and grow in the willingness to accept responsibility as a part of leadership. Leadership is the availability, attitude, aptitude, actions, alignment, assessment, and authority that are utilized to fulfill a project or assignment. I had to make myself available, and I had to have the proper attitude to do such a big assignment. I have a natural aptitude for these types of assignments. I knew I was going to enjoy the challenge of using my ability and training to take down that structure. Action is what had to be done with no more delays. Getting things in proper alignment was not a suggestion; it was a mandate. Assessing the problem was necessary to count the cost of this endeavor. I was given the authority to oversee the project to completion, which gave me the freedom to act without hindrance. I received permission from

the family and applied for the burn permit, which gave me permission from the fire department to burn shrubs, and the demolition permit from the county to tear down the structure.

Walking in excellence is about going through a process of refining your life and abilities and crafting your skills so that you can make the greatest impact for God's kingdom. Marks of excellence include getting your body in good physical shape and having the stamina to complete God's assignments.

Learning to interact with people and clearly communicate goals and plans is another key excelling principle. Competence and getting people who are excellent in their area of skills is vitally necessary to excel. Developing the discernment to understand what is needed, the personnel needed, and the timing of a task is key to succeeding in task and endeavors. Using technical tools and computers to maximize exact measurement helps projects be completed with exact specifications. You also need people skills and communication skills to connect with people. Excelling is learning to flow in the culture without compromising your convictions, being cool, calm, collected, and being a composed leader who impacts generations.

As husband and wife, we must recognize God's blessings, realize we excel when we help our families excel, and understand the heritage of true life and family.

> How joyful are those who fear the Lord—all who follow His ways! You will enjoy the fruit of your labor. How joyful and prosperous you will be! Your wife will be like a fruitful grapevine flourishing within your home. Your children will be like rigorous young olive trees as they sit around your table. That

> is the Lord's blessing for those who fear him.
> May the Lord continually bless you from
> Zion. May you see Jerusalem prosper as
> long as you live. May you live to enjoy your
> grandchildren. May Israel have peace. (Psalm
> 128:1–6 NLT)

I praise God that the Lord has allowed and is allowing us to experience the promises of this text. God is truly faithful.

To leave a legacy of excellence, a family must have the proper building materials and a proper foundation. Life happens, trials will come, and unimaginable challenges will come, but if the house is built upon the rock, the home will stand the test of time (Luke 6:47–49 NLT). We must listen and follow God's teachings, which is a solid foundation for your family. Many families are collapsing and are in ruins because they will not hear and obey God's Word, will, and ways.

If it had not been for the grace of God upon my marriage and family, we would have been destroyed and ruined. I thank God for giving us the desire and heart to live by His Word, which has been the catalyst for our marriage in 1987 and the blessings of children and grandchildren. I am certainly humbled by God's mercy and grace upon our family. I ask for God's continual grace and divine preservation as we move into the future. I do not know what life challenges we will face, but my hope and faith remains in God to watch over my family in Jesus's name.

> Only I can tell you the future before it even
> happens. Everything I plan will come to pass,
> for I do whatever I wish. (Isaiah 46:10 NLT)

The purpose of the family is to reflect God's character; therefore, each family member reveals glimpses of God's plan. The man is placed as the foundation of the family because he was made from earth, and his role is to communicate with God and receive guidance in leading and training in the principles that encourage the family. His role is to pray, protect, provide, and prepare the family to live to honor God and to be productive citizens in society. He is to elevate his family to be successful in their calls and purposes.

The wife is to reflect God's nurturing character. She is to communicate with God as well, coming into agreement and partnership with God's plan for their family. This will reveal God's loving care and bring comfort to each family member (Proverbs 31 NLT). The children reflect how we are designed to respond.

Both parents must teach, train, and discipline their children to be obedient and respectful. Parents must discern how to discipline each child according to their bent, calling, and gifts. Parents must live by example and teach their children to live to glorify God. Whatever is given by God is a gift, and with this gift comes the responsibility to be good stewards of His gifts. We are to help our children recognize that they have a divine purpose and destiny. If they get off course or track and become derailed by life choices, we must pray for them and place them in the hands of Jesus.

> I have told you all this so that you may have peace in Me. Here on earth, you will have many trials and sorrow. But take heart because I have overcome the world. (John 16:33 NLT)

111

When the family follows God's blueprint, they are set up to excel. It is time for families to excel because we are at war with the culture that is trying to redefine the family. The family must bring God's favor back, seasoning the culture with light and truth. When the family is in order, there is an endowment of favor with God.

To excel personally, I have lived by four principles, and I always look for like-minded leaders. I call them the facts of life. We must be faithful to God and our families. We must make ourselves available to God in prayer and to our families. We must learn to live Christlike through all seasons of life. Lastly, we must continue to be in a learning mode so God can teach us new things going from faith to faith, strength to strength, and from glory to glory.

Seven Points of Excelling

1. Excelling and enthusiasm go hand in hand.
2. Excelling helps emancipate others.
3. Excelling is the embodiment of what God created you for.
4. Exceling helps you elevate to new horizons.
5. Excelling inspires others to excel.
6. Excelling bestows more abilities upon you from God.
7. Excelling enlightens, entertains, empowers, and exemplifies your exceptional ability to execute.

Excelling Moments

As a freshman at Western Carolina University, I felt like a deer in the headlights while I was learning the ways of college life and college athletics. I was learning the system, practicing long and rigorous hours, learning the names of my teammates, and learning the names of all the coaches on offense and defense.

I also had to learn the pecking order and who was there to get an education and who was there just to play sports—and teach their fellow players from different cultures how to party, get drunk, and get high.

As a freshman, I excelled and was recognized for my ability and speed on the first day. I was soon recognized as someone who did not use drugs or alcohol, and my teammates quickly noticed I did not use profanity. As a result, I stood out among my team. I did things—not on purpose—that catapulted me to the center of the team. One very funny moment happened on a game day. We were doing a walk-through with the plays in our polo shirts and khakis, and then we were on to a pregame meal. We were on the grass, and I intentionally moved toward the area that would position me at the front so I could get to the cafeteria ahead of the ninety-plus team members and coaches. When Coach said, "Okay, let's go eat," I headed out in front of the team and stepped on a snake that I had not noticed. I was so shocked by the snake that my normal voice changed to a higher pitch, which made all the members of the team take notice. Then came a roar of laughter as they saw my reaction and the change in my voice!

Another instance came during football practice. I was not aware that the first-team offense went against the second- and third-team defense and that first-team defense went against the second- and third-team offense. For some reason, I thought the first-team offense went against first-team defense. So, on a hot August day in Cullowhee, North Carolina, I was on the third-team offense and sometimes ran plays with second-team offense. As we began, I felt at ease running plays and making extra yardage on each run. I was having so much fun running the ball, and I felt unstoppable. I thought I was going against the third-team defense.

My coaches were excited and confirmed how well I was running the ball.

Another running back whispered, "Do you know who is over there?"

I said, "Yes, the third-team defense."

He said, "No, that is the first-team defense."

I said, "No way!"

The defensive coach was screaming at the first-team defense. He said, "How can you allow this freshman to run all over you like this?"

They were boiling hot and terribly angry. I had no idea that Louis Cooper, a furious defensive end who later went pro with the Kansas City Chiefs; Clyde Simmons, who later went pro with the Philadelphia Eagles; and Tiger Green, who later went pro with the Green Bay Packers were all over there. I could not believe I had excelled against one of the top defenses in the conference. I knew they would want to take me out at the next practice, and I did not help myself because I was not supposed to run the football like that on a top-notch defensive team. During the next practice, they did a job on me. Clyde Simmons hit me so hard on one play that I almost flipped. To excel, you must block out everyone and everything that keeps you from excelling. You have permission to excel regardless of who is on the other side trying to oppose you.

Because of my history with anger, many people felt I would fail. Some people even said my marriage and family would be destroyed. Those who opposed me failed to realize that I knew I was nothing without Christ and that I could not succeed without God's help. When difficult seasons come, I have learned to turn to God and entrust Him with the outcome. I trust God with myself, my marriage, and my family. He is my source for excelling. If I did not put my faith and trust in God, I would fail miserably. I give God all the glory for the great things He has done in my life. I am incredibly grateful for the Lord fighting for me over the decades:

> The Lord Himself will fight for you. Just stay
> calm. (Exodus 14:14 NLT)

Prayers to Excel

1. "He was the one prayed to the God of Israel, 'Oh, that you would bless me and expand my territory! Please be with me in all that I do and keep me from all trouble and pain!' And God granted him his request" (1 Chronicles 4:10 NLT).

2. "Teach us to realize the brevity of life, so that we may grow in wisdom" (Psalm 90:12 NLT).

3. "Satisfy us each morning with your unfailing love, so we may sing for joy to the end of our lives" (Psalm 90:14 NLT).

4. "Let us your servants, see you work again; let our children see your glory" (Psalm 90:16 NLT).

5. "And may the Lord our God show us his approval and make our efforts successful. Yes, make our efforts successful" (Psalm 90:17 NLT).

6. "For every child of God defeats this evil world, and we achieve this victory through our faith" (1 John 5:4 NLT).

7. "For the Lord your God is going with you! He will fight for you against your enemies, and he will give you victory" (Deuteronomy 20:4 NLT).

CLOSING

We have a great responsibility to look out for the well-being of the next generation.

> But if you cause one of these little ones who trusts in me to fall into sin, it would be better for you to be thrown into the sea with a large millstone hung around your neck. (Mark 9:42 NLT)

As parents and leaders, we must understand that our habits, language, attitudes, values, and priorities have a direct and an indirect influence upon the younger generations. We must remember that our children, grandchildren, and great-grandchildren will benefit from our decisions—or experience the consequences of our willful actions that are opposed to God's will. Obviously, none of us are perfect, and we will make mistakes, but willful and clear disobedience to God's design will impact His plan for the next generation and many future generations.

Understanding behaviors and watching for warning signs in our young people is so important. According to some experts, pressure is handled in five different ways. One way is by numbing oneself with the use of drugs and alcohol. Second is the feeling of abandonment. The third way is through hedonism—the "party until you drop" mentality. Fourth is when a person withdraws into role-playing games. Fifth is totally unplugging from life by suicide. The best thing we can do for our children is to spend quality and quantities of time with them. They may act like they do not like it, but they need it and want to spend time with their parents. Be intentional to plan healthy moments with loved ones, including game nights, family vacations, and holidays. Go the extra mile to celebrate birthdays, and anniversaries. God, our spouses, and our children are the most valuable treasures we have in life.

What has the Lord been speaking to you? God is speaking, but are you listening?

> For God speaks again and again, though people do not recognize it. He speaks in dreams, in visions of the night, when deep sleep falls on people as they lie in their beds. He whispers in their ears and terrifies them with warnings. (Job 33:14–16 NLT)

We must develop a voracious hearing ability, which means to be precisely accurate in hearing and seeing what God desires.

God seals instructions inside of us and has given us skills to fulfill the purpose we were born to complete.

> God arms me with strength, and He makes my way perfect. (Psalm 18:32 NLT)

We must have foresight from God so that we can stay on a smooth path and the highway of God, which helps us accelerate His purpose in our lives. Farsightedness means seeing ahead and knowing in advance. God gives insights as we seek the ability, and He gives us direction to go a specific way and fulfill a specific purpose that we have been designed for. God had you on His mind even before you were born.

Why do I write books? I am on a mission to educate a generation about the ways of God. My mission is to challenge leaders to seek God daily, live with transparency and integrity, and equip leaders with resources so that they can navigate through life by solving problems with excellence.

It is time for you to elevate and excel for the Lord. Philippians 2 includes seven clear directives from the apostle Paul. Number one is learning to live in harmony with yourself and accept who you are and the abilities God has bestowed upon you. Do you love yourself? If you do, that is awesome; it frees you to love others. If your answer is no, then you must ask, "Why not?" Is it because of decisions you have made or something you been told by others?

Harmony means flowing in the rhythm of your design and fulfilling your unique destiny with your personality, preferences, problems, passion, and purpose.

You must work out your salvation with fear and trembling. What does that mean? It requires work to make our way through issues with the understanding that God is observing us. He desires that we make the right decisions with humble hearts. It is the epitome of Micah 6:8 (NLT):

> No, O people, the LORD has told you what is good, and this is what he requires of you: to do what is right, to love mercy, and to walk humbly with your God.

We must do this amid a crooked and perverse generation.

You must do everything without grumbling and complaining. Life is too short; God desires us to be content and thankful.

> Be thankful in all circumstances, for this
> is God's will for you who belong to Christ
> Jesus. (1 Thessalonians 5:18 NLT)

Complaining limits you and displeases God, but thankfulness pleases God.

You must shine like stars in the world. Let your light shine brightly for Jesus. Do you ever wonder why you want to be a star? It is because God has instilled that in you. So, you have divine permission to be yourself and shine whether you are black, white, Italian, Greek, Asian, Latino, or Indian—or anything else!

> Rejoice, have the joy in your heart; this
> provides strength and vitality to your being.
> (Nehemiah 8:10 NLT)

Obey God. He has your best interests in mind, and He has your back. Our obedience positions us for amazing blessings and provision that is out of this world. Our obedience helps advance God's kingdom and point people to Jesus (Isaiah 1:19 NLT).

You must be blameless and harmless. Live to glorify God and help the cause of Christ by helping people find the source of life. His Name is Jesus.

Undisciplined leaders will face unnecessary hardships:

> A person without self-control is like a city with
> broken-down walls. (Proverbs 25:28 NLT)

Take my yoke upon you. Let me teach you, because I am humble and gentle of heart, and you will find rest for your souls. For my yoke is easy to bear, and the burden I give you is light. (Matthew 11: 29–30 NLT).

Opening Prayer over Your Life

Father, I come to you in the name of Jesus to plead His blood over my life, on all that belongs to me, and on all that over which You have made me steward. I plead the blood of Jesus on the portals of my mind, my body, my emotions, and my will. I believe the blood of the Lamb, which gives me access to the holy of holies, protects me. I plead the blood over my children and all those You have given me in this life. Lord, You have said that the life of the flesh is in the blood. Thank You for the blood that has cleansed me from sin and sealed the new covenant of which I am a partaker in Jesus's name. Amen.

Praying for Your Wife

1. I pray that you give my wife the fulfillment of knowing you in a deeper and richer way and help her be diligent and steadfast in her walk with you in Jesus's name.
2. Lord, I thank You for giving my wife a sound mind and discernment between good and evil, yielding to Your Word, will, and way in Jesus's name.
3. Lord, I pray that my wife understands that she can do all things through You in Jesus's name.
4. I pray my wife is calm and that you soothe her soul and give her your peace that passes all knowledge and understanding. Thank You for giving her balance in her body and give her inner tranquility—no matter what is happening around her in Jesus's name.
5. Father, establish in us bonds of love that cannot be broken. Show me how to love my wife in an ever-deepening way that she can clearly perceive. Enable

my wife and me to forgive each other quickly and completely in Jesus's name.

6. Lord, I lift my wife to you today and ask you to be in charge in her life. Please show her how to seek You first in all things and make time with You her priority every day. Help my wife to make our home a peaceful sanctuary.

7. Lord, I pray that You surround my wife with Your hand of protection. Keep her safe from any harmful thing, help my wife be disciplined in the care of her body, and show her how to make the right choices in Jesus's name.

Praying for Your Children and Grandchildren

1. "He was the one who prayed to the God of Israel, 'Oh, that you would bless me and expand my territory! Please be with me in all that I do and keep me from trouble and pain! And God granted him his request'" (1 Chronicles 4:10 NLT).

   Father, we pray that You will bless and expand our children and grandchildren's territory with opportunities that will advance Your kingdom and that You keep them from trouble and pain in Jesus's name.

2. "Your word is a lamp to guide my feet and a light for my path" (Psalm 119:105 NLT).

   Father, we pray that You will be a guiding light to our children and grandchildren and that they will follow Your path and purpose for their lives in Jesus's name.

3. "'For I know the plans I have for you,' says the LORD. 'They are plans for good and not for disaster, to give you a future and a hope'" (Jeremiah 29:11 NLT).

Father, we thank You for your promise to give our children and grandchildren good plans and not disastrous ones and to give them hope in the future a divine destiny in Jesus's name.

4. "So we have not stopped praying for you since we first heard about you. We ask God to give you complete knowledge of His will and to give you spiritual wisdom and understanding" (Colossians 1:9 NLT).

Father, we thank You for giving our children and grandchildren clear and complete knowledge of Your will—and that you will give them spiritual discernment and wisdom to understand all things in Jesus's name.

5. "All scripture is inspired by God and is useful to teach us what is true and to make us realize what is wrong in our lives. It corrects us when we are wrong and teaches us to do what is right. God uses it to prepare and equip his people to do every good work" (2 Timothy 3:16–17 NLT).

Father, we thank You that Your Word inspires our children and grandchildren. We also thank You that Your word helps them see right from wrong and helps them to receive correction. We also thank You that Your Word equips them to live successful and abundant lives in Jesus's name.

6. "I pray that your love will overflow more and more, and that you will keep on growing in knowledge and understanding. For I want you to understand what really matters, so that you may live pure and blameless lives until the day of Christ's return. May you always be filled with the fruit of your salvation—the righteous character produced in your life by Jesus

Christ—for this will bring much glory and praise to God" (Philippians 1:9–11 NLT).

Father, we thank You that our children and grandchildren overflow with love and that they are filled with knowledge and understanding so that they know what truly matters in life—and that You will empower them to live purely and blamelessly throughout their lives. Fill our children, spouses, grandchildren, and entire family with Your salvation, which produces a life that is surrendered, sold out, and submitted to You in Jesus's name.

7. "Trust in the Lord with all your heart; do not depend on your own understanding. Seek his will in all you do, and he will show you which path to take" (Proverbs 3:5 NLT).

Father, help our children and grandchildren place their complete trust in You and help them do this with their whole hearts and learn to depend on You and seek You for guidance so that they know what decisions to make and the paths to take in Jesus's name.

Father, we thank you that our family live under the protection of your wings. We trust solely in you for safety and security. Lord, we thank you that you rescue us from the traps and schemes of the enemy, from every plague and every deadly disease. Your feathers and wings are our armor and protection. We do not have to be afraid of anything, for our faith is in you. Thank you for divine assistance from your angelic host. We thank you for commanding to angels to assist us when we are in danger and they come to the rescue quickly in Jesus's name. (Psalm 91:1–16 NLT)

I am a big John Wayne fan, and *El Dorado* is one of my favorite movies. The character John Wayne plays in the movie places high values on friendship, helps his friend through several predicaments, and works to help a friend through the good, bad, and ugly moments of life. This poem shows me how as we go through life's ups and downs, we are searching for friendship and purpose. Ultimately, we will join the heavenly host who are cheering us on in our journey of faith. In this journey to glory, we are to be bold in sunshine and shadow, when young and when old, through the mountains of the moon.

This poem by Edgar Allan Poe is sung and referred to throughout the movie:

> Gaily Bedight, a gallant knight, in sunshine and in shadow, had journeyed long, singing a song, in search of Eldorado. But he grew old, this knight so bold, and o'er his heart a shadow fell, as he found no spot of ground that looked like Eldorado. And as his strength failed him at length, he met a pilgrim. "Shadow," said he, "Where can it be this land of Eldorado?" "Over the mountains of the moon, ride, boldly ride," the shade replied, "if you seek for Eldorado!"

I had always wondered if John Wayne ever received Christ. Vickie and I were invited to attend a "Men with a Purpose" luncheon with our friend Craig Johnston, and that was where we heard the wonderful story of how John Wayne received Christ.

John Wayne was a big fan of Reverend Robert Schuller, an American Christian televangelist, who was famous for his weekly "Hour of Power" TV Program from 1970 until 2010. On one of the programs, the Duke heard Dr. Schuller say that his daughter Cindy had been in a terrible motorcycle accident and had to have her leg amputated. John Wayne wrote a note to her: "Dear Cindy, I am sorry to hear about your accident. Hope you will be all right." He signed it, and the note was delivered to her.

Cindy read it immediately and decided she wanted to write John Wayne a personal note:

> Dear Mr. Wayne,
>
> I got your note. Thanks for writing to me. I like you very much. I am going to be all right because Jesus is going to help me. Mr. Wayne, do you know Jesus? I sure hope you know Jesus, Mr. Wayne, because I cannot imagine heaven being complete without John Wayne being there. I hope, if you don't know Jesus, that you will give your heart to Jesus right now. See you in heaven.
>
> Cindy Schuller

Cindy put that letter in an envelope, sealed it, and wrote his name across the front.

A visitor came to her room and said, "What are you doing?"

She said, "I just wrote a letter to John Wayne, but I don't know how to get it to him."

The visitor said, "That's funny. I am going to have dinner

with John Wayne tonight at the Newport Club in Newport Beach. Give it to me, and I will give it to him."

Cindy gave him the letter, and he put it in his coat pocket.

That night, twelve people were sitting around the table for dinner. They were laughing and cutting up, and the visitor happened to reach in his pocket and feel the letter.

John Wayne was seated at the end of the table, and the guy took out the letter and said, "Hey, Duke, I was in Reverend Schuller's daughter's hospital room today. She wrote you a letter and wanted me to give it to you. Here it is."

They passed it down to John Wayne, and he opened it. They kept on laughing and cutting up, and someone happened to look over at John Wayne. He was crying.

Someone said, "Hey, Duke what's the matter?"

He said, "I want to read you this letter." He read it out loud and began to weep again. He folded the letter, put it in his pocket, pointed to the man who had delivered it, and said, "You go tell that little girl that right now, in this restaurant, right here, John Wayne gives his heart to Jesus Christ and will see her in heaven."

Three weeks later, John Wayne died!

You simply never know how giving witness to another person may affect their eternity!

> For I am not ashamed of the Gospel, because it is the power of God that brings salvation to everyone who believes: first to the Jew, then to the Gentile. For in the Gospel the righteousness of God is revealed a righteousness that is by faith from first to last, just as it is written: The righteous will live by faith. (Romans 1:16–17 NKJV)